Jesus Said It

"... teach these new disciples to obey
all the commands I have given you."
Matt. 28:20

Derek Gerrard

Jesus Said It

Published by BTC Publishing
a division of Local Community Church Ltd
PO Box 403 Scarborough WA 6922
Australia

ISBN 978-0-9874141-4-4 (print)
ISBN 978-0-9874141-5-1 (eBook)

www.derekgerrard.com
www.localcommunity.church

*This book is dedicated to all those people who are doing
their best to follow the things that Jesus said.*

*Thanks to my amazing wife for always supporting me in these
projects and for being an excellent editor.*

Thanks to Lachlan Scotford for the cover design.

Contents

Introduction
Jesus said what?

We are followers of Jesus – but what does that really mean? To follow a man who lived over 2,000 years ago, where His culture, language and heritage was so different from ours. In many ways, it doesn't make any sense and yet over a third of the world's population would say they follow the way of Jesus.

What makes it easier is doing that journey with a community of Christians – that's the church. The place where among other things, we get to figure this out together and put it into action in our lives.

A few years ago, our church spent a year studying around the theme in Matthew 28:19, where Jesus says to "go and make disciples". In other words, what does it look like to be followers of Jesus who make other followers of Jesus. After finishing the year with that, we were struck by the next verse in Matt. 28:20 where Jesus says that we should "teach these disciples to obey all the commands I have given you". So, we spent the following year unpacking all the commands that Jesus taught and that's a short history of how this book came about.

To follow Jesus ultimately means to follow what He says. When I read through the gospels and look at what He says, there are about fifty commands. I'm sure there might be theological scholars who will disagree around whether it is fifty, but it will take me a lifetime to learn how to live Jesus' two greatest commandments of loving God with all your heart, strength, soul and mind and then loving other people like you want to be loved yourself, so fifty is a pretty big ask to get through.

This book is a devotional that allows you to reflect on Jesus' fifty commands. In compiling this, there are things that I thought Jesus said that He never actually said and there are things that He said, which to be honest, I really don't like and wish He never said at all. To put some of these things into action is really hard.

Before we begin, we need to clarify a couple of things. If you're like me, the thought of following commands sounds too much like living by the rules. Being put in a box with constraints on living. It sounds too religious and rules are there for breaking anyway, so the very thought of following commands doesn't stir up feelings of a lifestyle I want to follow. Living these is our response to what Jesus has done for us. To live like Jesus is our worship. Our life and our actions should display evidence that we are following Jesus. We also need to remember that what Jesus said isn't about a set of rules to control our behaviour, but the best way to enjoy life and live it to the full. His way is the best way.

The revelation I've had about this set of commands is to remember it is for freedom that Jesus set us free (Gal. 5:1). What I've discovered is that by submitting my life to Jesus, letting Him genuinely be the Lord of my life and trying to follow His ways, His commands, I have found freedom. That thought seems so contradictory to begin with, but I hope on this journey, you discover something similar. Freedom is not found from a set of religious commands, but out of a desire to pursue Jesus, posturing your life after His, as a response of thanks for all that He has done in bringing salvation and eternal life.

Let's read what Jesus said about His own commands from John 14:23-26:

Jesus replied, "All who love me will do what I say. My Father will love them, and we will come and make our home with each of them. Anyone who doesn't love me will not obey me. And remember, my words are not my own. What I am telling you is from the Father who sent me. I am telling you these things now while I am still with you. But when the Father sends the Advocate as my representative - that is, the Holy Spirit - He will teach you everything and will remind you of everything I have told you."

What's great about this is His promise that we have the Holy Spirit, who will teach us and remind us of what Jesus said. That is my prayer for you as you go on this journey, that He will reveal what you need to hear at this point in your life. He goes on to say in John 15:10-11:

"When you obey my commandments, you remain in my love, just as I obey my Father's commandments and remain in His love. I have told you these things so that you will be filled with my joy. Yes, your joy will overflow!"

How good is that. If we follow His commands, we will be filled with joy. In a world searching for happiness, maybe we've just found the answer right here.

When we read a command of Jesus, we need to take it in context with the culture, the people and the issue He was speaking into at the time. You are likely to read the command from a modern translation of the Bible and need to realise that our way of thinking is based on a Greek philosophy that has been reshaped by Roman and Christian influences over the last 2,000 years. It defines our approach to economics, education, politics and community. While some of the Bible is written in Greek, we have an English translation, from Greek writings, applying our Greek, Roman, Christian worldview into a culture and history that was entirely Hebrew.

The Hebrew worldview was radically different from the Greek worldview and understanding these differences can help us get a better understanding of what Jesus was trying to say and how we might apply it to our lives.

I'll try and help explain this as we go through, but at a high level, the Hebrew worldview is that God is the main player in the universe. Everything revolves around Him, His purpose, His will and His control. The heritage of our worldview is that humans are the central player in the world. Humans' goals, creations, abilities and decisions are the most important aspects of the world. Obviously very different starting positions, so being aware of this will help.

GETTING THE MOST OUT OF THIS BOOK
You can read this book straight through as a fifty-day Bible Reading Plan, but it is intended as a year-long devotional. There are fifty chapters, basically one chapter for each command, one chapter for each week. While you may only read one Scripture for the week, I suggest you re-read it each day. Look at different translations, do further research around the command and spend some time meditating on what Jesus was saying.

I've included the main Scripture reference from both the New Living Translation (NLT) and The Message (MSG) which aims to put the Bible in contemporary language. I've cross-referenced other parts of the Gospels where Jesus said the same or similar things that you can look up. Then I've also included a couple of pages to give you some thoughts around each command and, some questions to help you put that command into action in your life. I hope you enjoy exploring the things that Jesus said and learning how you put them into action in your life.

One

Live on the word of God

Key Reference: Matt. 4:4
Other References: Luke 4:4

NLT
*"People do not live by bread alone,
but by every word that comes from the mouth of God."*

MSG
*"Jesus answered by quoting Deuteronomy: 'It takes more than bread to stay alive.
It takes a steady stream of words from God's mouth'."*

It's great that Jesus' first command is letting us know how important it is to live by His words.

When Jesus is referring to "the Word" there is both the written word (logos) and the spoken word (rhema).

The written word (logos) is the Bible. We are fortunate that we are able to easily access the Bible. The early followers of Jesus did not have their own copy of the Scriptures and would usually have to go to public readings to listen to the written word being read. It's almost like we have an advantage these days. If you struggle to read the Bible, it is worth persevering to find a way to learn to love it – after all, it is the written word of God.

The Bible is the best-selling book of all time (it's more a collection of books). The Bible Society estimates that over the last 150 years at least 6 billion copies have been printed and it has been translated into over 2,500 languages. It's an amazing book that was written over a 1,500 year period, from 1,400BC to 100AD. It was written by over 40 authors from all walks of life, covering 40 generations and written on three continents of Africa, Asia and Europe.

It contains history, poetry, songs, biographies and letters with topics on creation, relationships, love, war, money, property, music, parties, weddings and the future.

Paul writes, "all Scripture is inspired by God..." (2 Tim. 3:16) and there are many other Scriptures that talk about meditating on the Bible (take a look at Joshua 1:8 and Psalm 1:2-3 as examples).

The spoken word (rhema) is about realising that the Bible reveals God but doesn't limit God. In other words, He will continue to speak today in ways that are consistent with what we read in the Bible. John 14:26 says that the Holy Spirit is the Father's representative who will teach us and remind us of everything that Jesus has told us.

The Holy Spirit will speak to you – we just need to learn how to listen. That could be through those quiet thoughts in your mind, through words someone else speaks and other interactions in your life. When you accept Christ, you receive the Holy Spirit – so we need to trust that He is God and learn how to hear Him.

As we hear God, we also need to be prepared to obey what He says. In Luke 11:28 Jesus says, "even more blessed are all who hear the word of God and put it into practice".

ACTION

What are some of the most impacting things you can recall that God has spoken to you, either through the written form of the Bible or a spoken form? What patterns can you put in your life to regularly have a "steady stream of words from God's mouth"?

Two
Don't test God

Key Reference: Matt. 4:7
Other References: Luke 4:12

NLT
Jesus responded, "The Scriptures also say,
'You must not test the Lord your God'."

MSG
Jesus countered with another citation from Deuteronomy:
"Don't you dare test the Lord your God".

To understand what this command is about, we need to track through Scripture and go back to where the original command was given. Read Exodus 17:1-7 and you will see that the Israelites were in the wilderness for a period of trial and testing after being led out of Egypt. At this point they were thirsty and demanding water. Despite the slavery they had come from, they were starting to question why they had been saved, given the conditions they were living in and the trials they were now facing.

The Israelites were testing God to see if He would continue to provide for them, as if parting the Red Sea, releasing them from slavery and providing food in the form of manna, was not enough. They were basically saying - prove to us that you are God and that you care for us. They challenged God, despite evidence to the contrary. Moses called the place where this happened "Massah", which means "test". They believed that God should act according to their will. Their faith depended on what God would do for them – not on who God was (sound familiar?).

Even though God was not happy with their attitude, He provided the water, but shortly after this, God gave His commands (Deut. 6), which if obeyed by the Israelites, came with the promise of a long life and that all would go well with them. As part of that He said, "You must not test the Lord your God as you did when you complained at Massah."

So then in Matthew with Jesus, He is facing the devil, who was asking Him to prove that God was with Him. For each one of the devil's temptations, Jesus had an answer from Scripture and His final response was to refer to this original command, that we must not test the Lord our God, and it is this second command of Jesus that we are exploring.

This context is important, as it is a foundational truth of trust, faith and God's sovereignty. God has done everything He needs to do – and yet He is still involved in our lives, caring for us. How He shows this care though, is His choice, and that's where we need to trust His sovereignty.

In times of difficulty we can find ourselves praying that prayer "God if you can just do this, then I will really believe that you are there." This is the test that Jesus is referring to. We don't need to get God to prove that He is God.

He is our Father and so He loves to take care of us and always knows what is best for us, so we don't need to put Him to the test. All of us at times have circumstances that create struggles. It's often easy to feel like God is not there, that He is distant and doesn't care. To not test God, means we should not look at God through our circumstances, but look at our circumstances through God. Just by flipping that lens, it can help us realise that God is always doing something in the challenges of our life. It helps us recall the things he's done in the past and build faith, that He is in our future.

That shift in perspective allows us to recall His promises and look for the truth of them in the situation we're dealing with. Promises like, He will never leave us or forsake us, that we can do all things in Christ who strengthens us, and that if He is for us then who can be against us.

ACTION
What are you trusting God for right now in your life?
How are you trusting God in that situation without testing Him?
What things has God done in your past, that helps you build faith that He is in your future?

Three
Worship God only

Key Reference: Matt. 4:10
Other References: Luke 4:8

NLT
Jesus told him. "For the Scriptures say,
'You must worship the Lord your God and serve only him'."

MSG
He backed His rebuke with a third quotation from Deuteronomy: "Worship the
Lord your God, and only him. Serve him with absolute single-heartedness."

It's amazing how Jesus' commands echo the commands of the Old Testament and in this case, it's the first command of the Ten Commandments. In Exodus 20:1-2, God says, "You shall have no other Gods before me".

Recognising that God is God, is what underpins all the other commands we are called to obey. We don't live aimlessly, following these as a moral benchmark, but we live them out as a response to the God who created us, loves us and wants the fullest possible relationship with us. When we put something before God, it becomes an issue of idolatry.

Worship is a human activity, not just something for Christians. As worshippers, we are divided into two categories – those who worship the creator and those who worship created things. Because of sin in the world, we tend to worship anyone and anything other than the God who created everything.

We can be attached to the physical, things we can see and touch, rather than the spiritual. When we make a created thing a God thing, this is idolatry. In other words, idolatry is anything in your life that competes with God and wins.

God wants to be at the centre of our lives. It doesn't mean that we don't enjoy His creation, in fact He wants us to enjoy it and often gives us gifts. It's just that these gifts can become idols, if they replace God at the centre of our life. Identifying idols can be challenging – but have a go at honestly answering these questions and see what shows up:

- what do you long for most?
- where do you go for comfort?
- what are you most afraid of?

- what do you brag about?
- what do you want to have more than anything else?
- whose approval are you seeking?
- what do you complain about?

If you recognise that you are prone to idol worship, meaning that your sinful tendency is to worship creation rather than the creator, then you can do something about it.

Firstly, recognise that the idol lies: money says security; career says status and success; relationship says completeness; possessions say happiness; beauty says acceptance. When in reality, these are empty, false promises.

The great news is that you can break the idols in your life. Repent that they have taken the place of God in your life and by God's grace allow His forgiveness to help you re-centre your life on Him. Sometimes it's good to share this with a trusted friend, to help you keep accountability to that change.

Finally, replace the idols in your life with God. As humans, we were created to worship, so we can't stop worshipping, but what we can do is turn to Jesus and worship Him.

ACTION
Were you able to have an honest reflection and identify any idols in your life? What steps can you take to replace those idols and put Jesus back at the centre?

Four

Repent for the kingdom of God is near

Key Reference: Matt. 4:17
Other References: Mark 1:15

NLT
From then on Jesus began to preach, "Repent of your sins and turn to God, for the Kingdom of Heaven is near."

MSG
He picked up where John left off: "Change your life. God's kingdom is here."

This is the core of the Gospel message: "Repent for the kingdom of God is near". Jesus said it many times, Peter said it (Acts 3:19) and Paul said it (2 Cor. 7:9-10).

What does the pattern of repentance look like in your life? When bad things happen to people, they often turn to God in a hope that their lives will improve. In those challenging times, our desires are not always based on God's perspective, but on our desire to remove the pain we are facing. There is often no long-term loyalty to God, no understanding of His heart and at worst, repentance can just become a quick prayer to remove the guilt of what we did.

The word "repent" comes from the Greek word metanoia. It literally means to reverse your direction, to do an about-face. Turning and going in the other direction involves a lot more than saying a quick prayer. It's about a change in attitude and in action.

Regret is not repentance. It is remorse for something you have done wrong. Regret says, "I wish I hadn't done what I did", but it is not the determination to never do it again. It is feeling sorry for your past behaviour, but it doesn't necessarily direct your future actions.

Repentance requires us to recognise what we have done wrong, confess it and then seek and accept forgiveness (1 John 1:9). So, what is it that we are meant to repent from? God's original intention was that humanity was to live in close relationship with Him. When we disobey God, it causes separation. This separation comes when we look to find meaning, purpose and fulfilment in places other than God. When we don't trust him, when we live our own way, this is what we call sin. This is what we need to repent from.

Repentance is only possible because of Jesus. He died to save us from our sins. Not to get too heavy, but the penalty for our sin is death, eternal death, and Jesus died on a cross to pay the penalty for us. His resurrection, overcoming sin and death, is what provides forgiveness for all of us and allows the relationship with Him to be restored.

Repentance never ends, and you will find there is an unending discovery of things in your life that need a change in direction. That's what is so great about journeying with God, there is always more. Repentance is a way of life, not a one-time event, and not something to be afraid of.

If we truly repent, then we understand the weight of what we have been forgiven from. The result should be a life that more and more reflects the character of Jesus as He forgives us: more love for others, more joy, more peace, patience and kindness.

Because repentance is about a reverse of direction, the only real sign of whether you have repented will be what you do when the opportunity to sin presents itself again. We get the chance to repeat the sin that we have been forgiven from, or to respond differently and go in the opposite direction.

ACTION

Take some time to allow God to shine a light on anything you need to repent from. Confess your sin, repent and accept His forgiveness.

Think about how you will do the opposite, the next time this sin presents itself.

Five

Come follow me

Key Reference: Matt. 4:19
Other References: Mark 1:17

NLT

*Jesus called out to them, "Come, follow me,
and I will show you how to fish for people!"*

MSG

*Jesus said to them, "Come with me.
I'll make a new kind of fisherman out of you."*

While Jesus' command here is to come and follow Him, to put this into practice is to be a disciple of Jesus, who makes other disciples of Jesus.

At the end of Jesus' ministry, we hear Him say to all of us to go and make disciples (Matt. 28:18). Paul sums this up well when He says, "Follow me as I follow Christ." Ultimately, we all follow Jesus, but the heart of discipleship is having someone follow you, as you follow Christ.

At the outset this is confronting, do we genuinely want someone to look at our life and use it as an example of what it means to follow Christ? It's a good checkpoint to examine our own life and make those changes we know we need to make.

When we read Jesus asking others to follow Him, we see His model for discipleship. We understand that Jesus was inclusive – but there was an aspect of His discipleship that was exclusive, in that He selected twelve men that He walked with very closely. The number needs to be this size, because there is a limit to how many people you can intentionally invest in.

So, what can we learn about how Jesus discipled, that we can put into practice as we become disciples who make disciples?

The first thing is that He chose His disciples. They were selected and He asked them to follow Him. Sometimes we need to be proactive when we call people into our world, to let them see how we follow Jesus. As an example of this, a few years ago I asked six friends to join me once a week on my daily prayer walk. We prayed together, but it was also a chance to let them see what my daily routine with the Lord looked like. Some of them have gone on and done the same thing with people they are discipling.

Jesus spent a lot of time with His disciples. They went to parties together, shared meals together, travelled together, fished together, prayed together and so on. This idea of doing life together, being with each other in the best and the worst of times and genuinely living out what it means to be in community, is such an important part of discipleship. In our modern cities, we often isolate from one another and so we need to be very intentional about spending time doing life together. Much of what Jesus taught came from these moments together and "class" was always on (see John 13:1-7 as an example). If all of our life is about Jesus, situations will naturally come up for discipleship.

Jesus often put His disciples in growth situations (see Luke 9:1-6). He considered those times where He had to set an example of how to respond to a situation, but at other times He let His disciples have a go. Sometimes they succeeded at this, but other times they failed. It was in these moments they learnt, which then equipped them to lead the expansion of the church once Jesus had ascended to heaven. Jesus' discipleship revolved around a mission for His disciples to complete.

When we are discipling someone, we need to determine which situations we are to set an example through and what are the situations where we step back and let them have a go. Consider this simple model of development that helps articulate this interaction: I do; I do, you watch; you do, I watch; you do.

Finally, He treated each one of His disciples as individuals. Think about the different relationships He had that we get insights into: He confronted Peter, loved John, challenged Thomas and tolerated Judas. We need to remember that each person we are discipling is an individual. They have a unique set of experiences, personality, heritage, skills etc. and our goal in discipling them is to help them be the best follower of Jesus that they can be.

ACTION

We all need to learn from one another – is there someone discipling you right now, and if not, who would you want that to be?

Are you discipling anyone now and if not, is there someone you could offer that to?

What practical things can you do when you are discipling someone?

Six
Rejoice and be glad

Key Reference: Matt. 5:11-12

NLT

"God blesses you when people mock you and persecute you and lie about you and say all sorts of evil things against you because you are my followers. Be happy about it! Be very glad! For a great reward awaits you in heaven. And remember, the ancient prophets were persecuted in the same way."

MSG

"Not only that - count yourselves blessed every time people put you down or throw you out or speak lies about you to discredit me. What it means is that the truth is too close for comfort and they are uncomfortable. You can be glad when that happens - give a cheer, even! - for though they don't like it, I do! And all heaven applauds. And know that you are in good company. My prophets and witnesses have always gotten into this kind of trouble."

Sooner or later as a Christian, you will be mistreated for the things you believe and the way you live your life. 2 Timothy 3:12 says, "Indeed all who desire to live a godly life in Christ Jesus will be persecuted." If you think about it, a life in Christ can often be a statement against other people's lives. If you are chasing sexual purity, you are challenging people's love of free sex. If you avoid drunkenness, your life is a statement against the love of alcohol. If you pursue self-control, your life speaks against addiction. If you live simply, you speak against luxury and excess. If you live humbly, you expose pride. If you show compassion, you reveal self-centredness. If you are spiritually minded, you expose worldly mindedness.

Here Jesus is saying to rejoice in the things that come against us – so how do we do that? Sometimes we need to shift our response to pain and suffering. We can have a belief that when we find Christ everything in our world will be good, but this is not scripturally true, in fact as we have read, it says that we will have suffering and persecution.

We can rejoice because our challenges create opportunities. Think about the biggest change you have made in your life. Now think about why you made that change. Often that happens because of pain. At the time the pain may have felt unbearable, but hopefully now it's behind you. It's often our sufferings that cause us to change for the better. (See Rom. 5:3-5 for some further exploration of this).

When we are talking about pain, I want to recognise those who may still be in a season of pain and suffering, because some pain can't be explained, and if that is a situation you are in, I am truly sorry for that. God is a good God, and in those moments, we often want to ask, "Why did God let that happen?". It's not something we can unpack here, but my encouragement is that when we are suffering, what we need more deeply and urgently than any answers... is God.

We can rejoice, because that's what Jesus did – we follow His example. In Hebrews 12:1-3 we read that He could deal with the sufferings in this world because He knew of the joy that was awaiting Him in heaven. Our reward is also in heaven. Jesus wants us to desire Him more than we desire the reward of this world and so we should never stop rejoicing in our salvation. This command to rejoice and be glad is about an attitude of thankfulness. It is good practice to have a regular pattern of thankfulness. Thankfulness helps keep you humble and helps you keep perspective. When you stop and think about what you're thankful for, it also gives you energy to spend time helping others who may be less fortunate than you.

Thankfulness also helps you build your relationship with God. The Message translation of the Bible says in Psalm 100 that to enter the presence of God – the password is thanks. If you are feeling distant from God, what a great way to find your way back to him, by thanking him for the things He has done for you. There are even studies that have proven the benefits of gratitude, improved energy levels, increased self-esteem, decreased stress and a heightened level of spirituality, with an ability to see something bigger than ourselves, so this command to rejoice and be glad is a great one to action every day.

ACTION
Are there times in your life you can recall where challenges have created opportunities for positive change?
What are three things you are thankful for today?

Seven
You are the salt of the earth

Key Reference: Matt. 5:13

NLT

"You are the salt of the earth, but if salt has lost its taste, how shall its saltiness be restored? It is no longer good for anything except to be thrown out and trampled under people's feet."

MSG

"Let me tell you why you are here. You're here to be salt-seasoning that brings out the God-flavours of this earth."

Today salt is in large supply and used mainly in food for flavouring, but to understand the context of what Jesus meant, we need to think about the use of salt in ancient historic times.

Salt was a lot more valuable then and at some points in history was even used as a method of trade and currency. You may recall the saying "not worth His salt", which was reference to the practice of trading slaves for salt in ancient Greece. Salt rations were given to Roman soldiers, known as "salarium argentum", which is the origin of the English word "salary".

Knowing this value of salt in Jesus' time, gives further meaning to what He meant by this command. To be the salt of the earth is about offering something that is priceless, something that people desire.

The way we live is meant to add value to the world, to the point that when people see us and the way we live, it is "attractive" and they enquire more. That could be our joy in all circumstances, our humility in putting others before ourselves, a care for all people irrespective of who they are, and the list goes on. The Cambridge dictionary literally translates "salt of the earth" as someone who is a very good and honest person.

Salt is essential in the diets of humans and animals. Salt, or sodium, is an element that causes the body to become thirsty by activating electrolytes. The water then allows the kidneys to distribute a healthy amount of electrolytes throughout the bloodstream, which in turn regulates blood pressure. So, by us being salt in the earth, it can create a thirst or a desire for others to want to know Jesus.

Salt is also one of the most effective and widely-used preservatives. A preservative prevents food getting spoiled, so our role in the world is to present the truth of Jesus to people, which if they follow, can protect them from eternal spoiling.

The analogy of salt continues because if salt remains in its container, it does not serve its purpose of preserving or flavouring. Likewise, if we remain contained, we do not serve the purpose we have in the world.

Finally, salt adds flavour and seasoning to the food to which it is added. We are meant to add colour and flavour, creativity and innovation to the interactions we have in the world. As The Message says, we "bring out the God-flavours of this earth."

Salt of the earth is like the next command of Jesus, "You are the light of the world", as they are both about us being Jesus' witness. Once you find Jesus and become His follower, your personal spiritual journey is important, but there is also a clear calling to tell others about Him.

Our life, our actions and our words are about advancing God's kingdom here on earth and this theme continues to run throughout the Gospels and into the writings of the New Testament.

ACTION
Where in the world are you being "salt"?
What can you practically do that means you are Jesus' witness?
Where in the world do you add colour and flavour, creativity and innovation?

Eight
You are the light of the world

Key Reference: Matt. 5:14-16

NLT

You are the light of the world—like a city on a hilltop that cannot be hidden. No one lights a lamp and then puts it under a basket. Instead, a lamp is placed on a stand, where it gives light to everyone in the house. In the same way, let your good deeds shine out for all to see, so that everyone will praise your heavenly Father."

MSG

Here's another way to put it: You're here to be light, bringing out the God-colors in the world. God is not a secret to be kept. We're going public with this, as public as a city on a hill. If I make you light-bearers, you don't think I'm going to hide you under a bucket, do you? I'm putting you on a light stand. Now that I've put you there on a hilltop, on a light stand—shine! Keep open house; be generous with your lives. By opening up to others, you'll prompt people to open up with God, this generous Father in heaven."

Where light exists, there can be no darkness. Paul references this well when He says, "So then let us cast off the works of darkness and put on the armour of light" (Rom. 13:12).

Everything living in a physical sense, depends on light in some way. We depend on food from plants, which partly get their food source from light or solar energy, so as humans we depend on the light.

So how do we become the light of the world, where light is the source of everything living? Ultimately Jesus is the light of the world (John 8:12) but like the moon has no light of its own and reflects the sun's light, so too are we meant to reflect the light of Christ. It's this reflection that allows us to become the light of the world.

There are three types of light that can represent three groups of people and three different ways we could be a light in the world – ways that we can be a witness.

Think of a room light – it is always on in the background, doing its job, it's consistent and warm. This is like the long-term relationships we have with family and friends. Our light should always be on, very consistent and over time, providing an example of what life looks like being a follower of Jesus. It could be described as relational evangelism, where we have many conversations about our faith over long periods of time, and the consistency of our actions provide a great example of living with Jesus.

Another type of light is a lighthouse. In the darkness, it is protecting ships from hitting danger, it is meeting a need. To be a light in the world like this we can think about acquaintances we have – work colleagues, neighbours, the hairdresser, people who run the local coffee shop etc and see if we can find a practical way to meet their needs. It is a great way to use practical love to demonstrate the love of God. Think of it as servant evangelism. Jesus refers to this in the command, "let your good deeds shine out for all to see".

The final type of light is lightning, it comes as a once off with power. This is an example of people we might only meet once in our life and we have one opportunity to give them the Gospel message right there. Think about a taxi driver or the stranger you sit next to on a plane.

These are all good deeds, because if we love people, we ultimately want to see them in relationship with Christ, so why not make the most of all the opportunities we have like this to be light and to share the Gospel. Whichever way you choose to be a light, it is about pushing back the darkness and advancing the kingdom of God.

ACTION

What are the different areas in your life you can be a light?
With those people, what good deeds can you do that demonstrate God's love to them?

Nine
Be reconciled

Key Reference: Matt. 5:21-24

NLT

"You have heard that our ancestors were told, 'You must not murder. If you commit murder, you are subject to judgment.' But I say, if you are even angry with someone, you are subject to judgment! If you call someone an idiot, you are in danger of being brought before the court. And if you curse someone, you are in danger of the fires of hell. So if you are presenting a sacrifice at the altar in the Temple and you suddenly remember that someone has something against you, leave your sacrifice there at the altar. Go and be reconciled to that person. Then come and offer your sacrifice to God."

MSG

"You're familiar with the command to the ancients, 'Do not murder.' I'm telling you that anyone who is so much as angry with a brother or sister is guilty of murder. Carelessly call a brother 'idiot!' and you just might find yourself hauled into court. Thoughtlessly yell 'stupid!' at a sister and you are on the brink of hellfire. The simple moral fact is that words kill. This is how I want you to conduct yourself in these matters. If you enter your place of worship and, about to make an offering, you suddenly remember a grudge a friend has against you, abandon your offering, leave immediately, go to this friend and make things right. Then and only then, come back and work things out with God."

When you put a group of people together from different backgrounds, with different experiences, different philosophies and ask them to do life in the context of a community – in our case the church – there are always going to be moments where there are strains on relationships. Often we call this conflict, and conflict is a natural part of humanity. While it is often presented as a negative thing, conflict can actually be very positive if it is handled in the right way.

Conflict facilitates the sharing of different viewpoints, which is partly how we learn. It allows us to understand more about ourselves regarding how we respond to certain situations. Conflict can be the catalyst to bring about healthy change. If people can navigate through conflict it can often strengthen their relationship. In fact, while it's nice to be agreeable all the time, if a relationship hasn't withstood conflict, the depth of that relationship could be shallow.

When someone does something against us, that causes hurt or offense, we always have a choice on how we will respond. Jesus clearly says here that we are to be reconciled to one another, and the importance of that is so great, that we should do that before we come and worship God.

In the church this is the concept of unity. It doesn't mean we think the same way or avoid conflict, but it does mean that we are joined as a whole. That we know the combination of us all together is better than us divided. That while we don't always agree, we're quick to forgive. A good way to think about unity in the church is around the context of community – or committed unity. Reconciled relationships are key to this. Commitment is happening less and less in our society where people leave their options open, but a functioning community has commitment. Commitment to the cause of Jesus, that we all have in common. Commitment that says I'm going to show up for the long term, in the good times and the hard times. Commitment where we pray for each other and let our actions speak louder than our words. This leads to a committed unity. Unity that means we honour one another and fight through the challenging times for the sake of relationship. The enemy loves to undermine us in this area and does so through the tactics of gossip and holding onto offense. The way we defend against this, the way that we stay reconciled, is to practice forgiveness.

This command of Jesus is an easy one to skip past as a simple saying, but to put into practice can be very difficult. In this command, Jesus literally says that before we come to worship God in a corporate sense in church, or in your own personal devotion, we should stop and think about any earthly relationships that need to be reconciled. I'm not sure many of us do that.

It should be that our churches are a place that non-believers find attractive – because of our love for one another. This gets very real when it comes to working hard to be reconciled in relationships, particularly when we feel we have been wronged. This is where we need to practice forgiveness (you can read more about forgiveness in devotion 38 - Forgive Others) and even though that can be hard, we know it works, because this is what Jesus has done with us for the sake of relationship.

ACTION

Can you think of a time where conflict has been a positive in your life?
Are there any relationships you have now that need to be reconciled?
Do you need to forgive someone who has done wrong to you?

Ten

Honour marriage

Key Reference: Matt. 19:4-9
Other References: Matt. 5:27-32, Mark 10:6-9

NLT

"Haven't you read the Scriptures?" Jesus replied. "They record that from the beginning 'God made them male and female.' And He said, 'This explains why a man leaves His father and mother and is joined to His wife, and the two are united into one.' Since they are no longer two but one, let no one split apart what God has joined together. Then why did Moses say in the law that a man could give His wife a written notice of divorce and send her away?" they asked. Jesus replied, "Moses permitted divorce only as a concession to your hard hearts, but it was not what God had originally intended. And I tell you this, whoever divorces His wife and marries someone else commits adultery—unless His wife has been unfaithful."

MSG

He answered, "Haven't you read in your Bible that the Creator originally made man and woman for each other, male and female? And because of this, a man leaves father and mother and is firmly bonded to His wife, becoming one flesh— no longer two bodies but one. Because God created this organic union of the two sexes, no one should desecrate His art by cutting them apart. "They shot back in rebuttal, "If that's so, why did Moses give instructions for divorce papers and divorce procedures?" Jesus said, "Moses provided for divorce as a concession to your hard heartedness, but it is not part of God's original plan. I'm holding you to the original plan, and holding you liable for adultery if you divorce your faithful wife and then marry someone else. I make an exception in cases where the spouse has committed adultery."

God created us to be in community and at the heart of community is relationship. The most intimate form of that relationship is marriage – but this command is not just for married people – it creates a conversation for singles, married and people that have been divorced, so let's touch briefly on each of these.

Singleness is often looked down upon in church circles and the focus can be on getting married, but throughout Scripture we read of encouragement to those who choose to be single for the sake of the kingdom. There are pros and cons of being single and of being married, and it is easy to focus on the things that we don't have rather than what we do have. Whether single or married we need to learn to enjoy the season we are in and use that for the sake of God's kingdom.

A friend of mine who is divorced but now lives in an amazing second marriage, once said to me that His reconciliation of this Scripture is that divorce is not what God intends, but God will still work through this situation and can still bring blessing. Our world is a place where most of us live with stuff that God didn't intend. Sometimes divorce is unavoidable because what has caused the divorce came from behaviour that was also not intended by God.

The key to building a great relationship and particularly a great marriage is through mutual sacrifice. "It's not about you" – means that in a relationship it is about service. It's about working on yourself for the benefit of others.

As a married person, I have to say that marriage is awesome and while this is not a book on building a better marriage, let me give you some thoughts that help take to heart what Jesus meant when He was saying, honour marriage.

Choosing your marriage partner is the most important decision you will make after following Christ. It's a love covenant for life and so impacts every part of your life thereafter. Marriage is about being your partner's biggest fan.

A great marriage is where the combination of both of you together is better than either individual. With Christ at the centre of a marriage there is a strong relationship that allows you to do great things to advance the Kingdom of God (read Eccles. 4:9-12 for a good analogy on this).

Marriage is an investment worth investing in. While there are seasons of hard work, there are also seasons of tremendous fruitfulness. In marriage, you need Jesus, as it's ultimately two sinners trying to do life together and you can't do it without Him at the centre.

Marriage is also the analogy Scripture uses as the relationship between Jesus, the bridegroom, and the church, His bride. Despite our flaws and shortcomings as the church, Jesus still loves us, laid down His life for us and is coming back for us. This incredible example of love is so true of marriage, where despite knowing our spouse's flaws and shortcomings, we can still love and fully accept them. The Gospel gives us the pattern for a great marriage.

ACTION
Do you need to change your perspective on singleness or marriage?
What can you apply from the heart of the Gospel message to doing relationships well?
What is the way God intends love to be, versus the way the world defines love?

Eleven
Keep your word

Key Reference: Matt. 5:33-37

NLT

"You have also heard that our ancestors were told, 'You must not break your vows; you must carry out the vows you make to the Lord.' But I say, do not make any vows! Do not say, 'By heaven!' because heaven is God's throne. And do not say, 'By the earth!' because the earth is His footstool. And do not say, 'By Jerusalem!' for Jerusalem is the city of the great King. Do not even say, 'By my head!' for you can't turn one hair white or black. Just say a simple, 'Yes, I will,' or 'No, I won't.' Anything beyond this is from the evil one."

MSG

"And don't say anything you don't mean. This counsel is embedded deep in our traditions. You only make things worse when you lay down a smoke screen of pious talk, saying, 'I'll pray for you,' and never doing it, or saying, 'God be with you,' and not meaning it. You don't make your words true by embellishing them with religious lace. In making your speech sound more religious, it becomes less true. Just say 'yes' and 'no.' When you manipulate words to get your own way, you go wrong."

Keeping your word is all about commitment and as we've previously reflected on, in this day and age commitment can be hard to find. We typically live in a world where people are less about commitment and more about keeping their options open. Part of the reason for this is because we have so many choices, and choices stop us committing. We don't commit to relationships because options tell us it's better to not become too involved. We don't commit to serving others because options tell us it might be better to keep our time to ourselves. We don't commit to giving our money away because options tell us we don't know what else we might need that money for, and the list goes on.

Keeping your word is about moving away from being a "maybe" person and becoming a committed person. Someone that commits early, keeps the commitment, shows up on time, has joy in what you are doing, even if you deem something better has come up. I'm sure you have been the recipient of someone letting you down, someone who has promised something but doesn't come through with the outcome. If you think about that situation and that person, it may be that you no longer trust them and don't rely on them. It would make sense then that Jesus has given this as a command. When it comes to living out our faith it is undermined if we do not keep our word.

There is power in the words that we use. The New Testament writer James expanded on this: "And a small rudder makes a huge ship turn wherever the pilot chooses to go, even though the winds are strong. In the same way, the tongue is a small thing that makes grand speeches. But a tiny spark can set a great forest on fire. And among all the parts of the body, the tongue is a flame of fire. It is a whole world of wickedness, corrupting your entire body. It can set your whole life on fire, for it is set on fire by hell itself." (James 3:4-6).

Keeping our word is both true of our relationship with Jesus and with one another. It's about being a person of integrity, being someone that is reliable and that people can trust. Not letting ourselves down, by letting others down. The most important word you can keep is the "yes" you say to following Jesus. Revelation talks about not being lukewarm in this decision, "I know all the things you do, that you are neither hot nor cold. I wish that you were one or the other. But since you are like lukewarm water, neither hot nor cold, I will spit you out of my mouth." (Rev. 3:15-16).

Throughout Scripture we see stories of people who said yes to Jesus, but also who said no to Him. Those that said "no" include the Rich Young Ruler (Mark 10:17-22), Judas Iscariot (Matt. 26:14-16) and Barabbas (Matt. 27:11-26). Then there are some great stories of those who said "yes" including Abraham (Gen. 12:1-4), Moses (Ex. 3:1-10) and Paul (Acts 9:1-20). So let's be people who keep our "yes".

ACTION

Can you think of times that you have not kept your word? What impact do you think that had on the person you let down?

What are some practical ways you can make sure you keep your word?

What do you need to shift to get back to the "yes" you said to follow Jesus?

Twelve

Turn the other cheek

Key Reference: Matt. 5:38-42

NLT

"You have heard the law that says the punishment must match the injury: 'An eye for an eye, and a tooth for a tooth.' But I say, do not resist an evil person! If someone slaps you on the right cheek, offer the other cheek also. If you are sued in court and your shirt is taken from you, give your coat, too. If a soldier demands that you carry His gear for a mile, carry it two miles. Give to those who ask, and don't turn away from those who want to borrow."

MSG

"Here's another old saying that deserves a second look: 'Eye for eye, tooth for tooth.' Is that going to get us anywhere? Here's what I propose: 'Don't hit back at all.' If someone strikes you, stand there and take it. If someone drags you into court and sues for the shirt off your back, giftwrap your best coat and make a present of it. And if someone takes unfair advantage of you, use the occasion to practice the servant life. No more tit-for-tat stuff. Live generously."

On a first read, this part of Jesus' Sermon on the Mount could be seen to imply pacifism, to accept whatever injustices or unfair treatment we experience. Jesus though, was also a bringer of truth and justice, so this command must be explored further to understand what Jesus is calling us to do.

To give some context we need to realise that in Jesus' time, the Roman Empire occupied the Israelite land, and the Roman soldiers were there to enforce their power and control. When a solder decided they wanted something from a Jewish person, it didn't make sense to resist. This could be to any number of things, including carrying the Roman soldier's load as they moved around – hence the reference to "if you have carried their gear for a mile – be prepared to take it for a further mile".

Jesus is referencing that we should not be people who retaliate. In the world, if someone has suffered an injustice, it's not uncommon that they will plan revenge, but to turn the other cheek means to act differently to this.

When we are faced with these types of injustices it's a chance to think about how we please God in the situation. That can be hard, because no one likes to be disrespected, but by responding with dignity it may open the door of respect. It shows a sign of strength to be able to respond by turning the other cheek.

Responding to the injustice with love might afford us the chance to share the Gospel. This type of response is an unnatural response, which in turn displays the supernatural power of the Holy Spirit within us. In Proverbs (Prov. 25:21-22) and Romans (Rom. 12:20), this is referred to as "heaping burning coals upon your enemies". It's almost an action that will shock the person doing evil towards repentance. To motivate those who abuse their power to change.

Practically speaking, it may be worth reflecting on why the person is hurting you in the first place. Is it in relation to pain inside them that they are responding to, trying to make themselves feel better and possibly something you can help them with? Alternatively, is it something that you have done that you need to look at seeking forgiveness from or making a change in your life?

As hard as this is, we know we can do it, because Jesus did it. He literally turned His cheek while He was suffering on the cross. He went through a slow and painful death at the hands of the Roman soldiers, while at the same time asking God to forgive them. He demonstrated limitless love for everyone. This is our example, to be as accommodating as we can for the sake of what it says to a lost world.

ACTION
Can you think of a time you sought revenge where you should have instead turned the other cheek?
How can you prepare yourself to turn the other cheek next time you face a situation of injustice?

Thirteen
Love your enemies

Key Reference: Luke 6:27-36
Other References: Matt. 5:43-48

NLT

"If you love only those who love you, why should you get credit for that? Even sinners love those who love them! And if you do good only to those who do good to you, why should you get credit? Even sinners do that much! And if you lend money only to those who can repay you, why should you get credit? Even sinners will lend to other sinners for a full return. Love your enemies! Do good to them. Lend to them without expecting to be repaid. Then your reward from heaven will be very great, and you will truly be acting as children of the Most High, for He is kind to those who are unthankful and wicked. You must be compassionate, just as your Father is compassionate."

MSG

"Here is a simple rule of thumb for behavior: Ask yourself what you want people to do for you; then grab the initiative and do it for them! If you only love the lovable, do you expect a pat on the back? Run-of-the-mill sinners do that. If you only help those who help you, do you expect a medal? Garden-variety sinners do that. If you only give for what you hope to get out of it, do you think that's charity? The stingiest of pawnbrokers does that. I tell you, love your enemies. Help and give without expecting a return. You'll never - I promise - regret it. Live out this God-created identity the way our Father lives toward us, generously and graciously, even when we're at our worst. Our Father is kind; you be kind."

A great place to start with this devotion is to think about the person in your life you dislike the most... and now pray for them. It probably feels very uncomfortable and yet this is what this command from Jesus is all about. It's more natural for us to avenge ourselves rather than loving our enemy, but it's hard to find happiness in life if you are carrying anything against someone else. The only way we can really do this is with the power of the Holy Spirit within us, leading us to follow the pattern that Jesus set. This command is one of the real distinctives of being a Christian.

While Jesus uses the word "enemies", we can consider not just "enemies", as that may not be the context you see someone in, but those people that are difficult to love. It is a good reminder to make sure you have difficult people in your life. We default to surrounding ourselves with similar people, those that we enjoy the company of. As Jesus points out in this command though, that is easy and anyone can do that, so we need to be intentional about having people in our life that are difficult to love. This is the Gospel message of loving all people.

You don't need to like your "enemy", or like what they do, but to love them is to be concerned for their welfare, to do things that will benefit them and not harm them.

We need to keep loving people when it hurts. It's about doing the long journey and not giving up, even when it feels like we aren't making any progress. We do this because Jesus never gave up on us. Even if people don't appreciate the love that we are showing them, God does.

How do you know if you really love your enemy? You pray for them. It's hard to hold offense or unforgiveness against someone you are praying for. It helps you see them more as Jesus sees them.

Once again, we can only do this because it is what Jesus has already done. He had enemies. He was physically abused, got spat on and lies were told about him. The religious people kept trying to catch him out and make fun of him. Even some of His friends turned their back on him. Peter denied Him, Judas betrayed Him and Thomas doubted Him, but through all of that, He chose to love.

To love others is our response to God first loving us. Paul wrote in Romans (Rom. 5:10), "For since our friendship with God was restored by the death of His Son while we were still His enemies, we will certainly be saved through the life of His Son. So now we can rejoice in our wonderful new relationship with God because our Lord Jesus Christ has made us friends of God."

We were once enemies of God, but because of Jesus, we are now friends of God.

ACTION
Do you have someone in your life that you find difficult to love?
How can you show love to those people that feel like your enemy?
Can you pray now for those you find hard to love?

Fourteen
Give to the needy

Key Reference: Matt. 6:1-4

NLT

"Watch out! Don't do your good deeds publicly, to be admired by others, for you will lose the reward from your Father in heaven. When you give to someone in need, don't do as the hypocrites do—blowing trumpets in the synagogues and streets to call attention to their acts of charity! I tell you the truth, they have received all the reward they will ever get. But when you give to someone in need, don't let your left hand know what your right hand is doing. Give your gifts in private, and your Father, who sees everything, will reward you."

MSG

"Be especially careful when you are trying to be good so that you don't make a performance out of it. It might be good theater, but the God who made you won't be applauding. "When you do something for someone else, don't call attention to yourself. You've seen them in action, I'm sure - 'playactors' I call them - treating prayer meeting and street corner alike as a stage, acting compassionate as long as someone is watching, playing to the crowds. They get applause, true, but that's all they get. When you help someone out, don't think about how it looks. Just do it - quietly and unobtrusively. That is the way your God, who conceived you in love, working behind the scenes, helps you out."

There are some people that only do good when they can be seen. Their goal is to be recognised for their generosity. Some of the greatest philanthropists of our time are like this. That's not to say their generosity isn't amazing, and in many cases has left a legacy that has achieved great things in our world. It's just that the reward for their efforts remain right here on earth.

Many of the religious leaders in Jesus' time made their giving very public. This was because this type of giving was about power. The religious leaders liked their benefits and without recognition of their wealth they thought they may lose these. If you supply another person's needs, and are recognised for doing so, the person you have given to will feel indebted to you. This creates a position of power as they accept your charity.

There are many examples of people giving throughout the New Testament, so what Jesus is saying isn't about an explicit command to make all your giving in secret, but that He cares about the intent or motive of your giving.

Our guiding principle should be giving privately, but it's mostly about your heart attitude as you give. This all assumes that you believe you should give, so let's just touch on that.

Giving is one of the most tangible ways we can worship God. It's about a heart attitude and a way of life, and not about the amount that you give. In our church at one end of the spectrum I have seen people give away cars, while at the other end I've seen children wrap up a coin with a note of encouragement on it and give it to a homeless person. The point is that it's the heart attitude that matters.

Perhaps you have experienced being the recipient of someone's giving and know how impacting that is. Likewise, if you have given something to someone, you will know it can also have a profound impact on you. It's the reality of what Jesus says: "it's more blessed to give than to receive". There are even studies that suggest giving makes you happier.

In my family, we have tried adopting a policy of "give while you live". In other words, not waiting until we've got more but giving now, helping others and seeing the difference it can make in people's lives.

Like so many of these commands our ultimate example lies in Jesus. God cared for us so much that He gave. He gave His son Jesus to pay the price for us, that means we can have eternal relationship with him. So, let's try to give to those most in need, just like Jesus did.

ACTION

Have you been the recipient of an unexpected gift? How did that make you feel?

When you have given in the past, what has been your heart motivation?

Can you adopt a life policy to give while you live?

Fifteen
Pray

Key Reference: Matt. 6:7-13
Other References: Luke, 11:1-4, Matt. 21:21-22

NLT

"When you pray, don't babble on and on as people of other religions do. They think their prayers are answered merely by repeating their words again and again. Don't be like them, for your Father knows exactly what you need even before you ask him! Pray like this: Our Father in heaven, may your name be kept holy. May your Kingdom come soon. May your will be done on earth, as it is in heaven. Give us today the food we need, and forgive us our sins, as we have forgiven those who sin against us. And don't let us yield to temptation, but rescue us from the evil one."

MSG

"The world is full of so-called prayer warriors who are prayer-ignorant. They're full of formulas and programs and advice, peddling techniques for getting what you want from God. Don't fall for that nonsense. This is your Father you are dealing with, and He knows better than you what you need. With a God like this loving you, you can pray very simply. Like this: Our Father in heaven, Reveal who you are. Set the world right; Do what's best - as above, so below. Keep us alive with three square meals. Keep us forgiven with you and forgiving others. Keep us safe from ourselves and the Devil. You're in charge! You can do anything you want! You're ablaze in beauty! Yes. Yes. Yes.

One of the key foundations of your relationship with Jesus is to pray and here Jesus is teaching us how to pray.

To break that down He begins with "Our Father". He could have started with Our King, or Our Creator, Our Lord, Our Friend, but it's Our Father – it's a family relationship. Our prayer life isn't meant to be a business or religious relationship but as children, adopted into the family of God.

John writes, "But to all who believed him and accepted him, He gave the right to become children of God. They are reborn—not with a physical birth resulting from human passion or plan, but a birth that comes from God." (John 1:12-13). This adoption changes our legal status and changes the way we pray.

He next says, "Hallowed be Your Name". This means sanctified, consecrated or set apart to be holy. It's about praise. From the depths of your heart, what is it that you praise God for?

"Your kingdom come, Your will be done, here on earth as it is in heaven." This is about submission. Believing that God's will is best, trusting that He is involved in our life despite the circumstances around us, but also believing for the goodness and victory of heaven to be evident in our lives on earth.

"Give us this day our daily bread" is about provision. We can ask God daily for the things that we need. In fact, we can go to God with every little thing in our life. As our Father He wants to hear from us and know what we desire. We can then trust Him with how He responds. As we do this, it's good to keep another of Jesus' teachings in mind – seek first the kingdom of God and all these things will be added unto you. In other words, while asking God for the things we want, we need to learn to prioritise that around things of the kingdom first.

"Forgive us our sins as we have forgiven those who sin against us". This is the time in our daily prayer for confession, repentance and forgiveness. To ask God to shine light on those things that we have done wrong, that we may repent, forgive ourselves and accept the forgiveness of Jesus so that we can reset again for the day ahead.

"Lead us not into temptation". This is about protection. Temptation is not sin, but when you give into temptation it becomes sin. We know God promises that He will not let us be tempted by more than we can bear, but it is good to realise we are in an ongoing battle and to commit to this prayer of protection.

One final piece of advice on prayer, is to find a prayer time and prayer place. Something that makes it a part of your daily routine, as it's the best way we find the presence of God and build relationship with Him.

ACTION
Can you build a regular prayer time and place into your daily routine?
Have you thought of structuring your prayer life on this model of Jesus?
Can you put this into practice and pray now?

Sixteen

Fast

Key Reference: Matt. 6:16-18

NLT

"And when you fast, don't make it obvious, as the hypocrites do, for they try to look miserable and disheveled so people will admire them for their fasting. I tell you the truth, that is the only reward they will ever get. But when you fast, comb your hair and wash your face. Then no one will notice that you are fasting, except your Father, who knows what you do in private. And your Father, who sees everything, will reward you."

MSG

"When you practice some appetite-denying discipline to better concentrate on God, don't make a production out of it. It might turn you into a small-time celebrity but it won't make you a saint. If you 'go into training' inwardly, act normal outwardly. Shampoo and comb your hair, brush your teeth, wash your face. God doesn't require attention-getting devices. He won't overlook what you are doing; he'll reward you well."

Food has become a real focus in our society. It's probably driven by all the cooking shows and the multi-million dollar industries built around health diets. Food can be an idol in our life and could be more of a focus for us than it was in Jesus time.

In a sense, everyone fasts. When we are in bed asleep, we go without any food or drink. That is fasting. That is why the first meal of the day is called breakfast – to break the fast. However, when we read of fasting like Jesus is referring to, it's a longer period of deliberately choosing not to eat and drink for a spiritual purpose.

That spiritual purpose could be needing to hear God's voice about a situation you are in, needing a breakthrough in healing for yourself or someone else, or to try and deal with habitual sin. There are so many areas that we might seek God for in a spiritual fast, but we need to remember it's always about seeking God.

During spiritual fasting, our focus is removed from the physical things of this world and intensely concentrated on God. Fasting directs our hunger toward God. It clears the mind and body of earthly attentions and draws us closer to God, allowing us to hear Him more clearly.

What Jesus is referring to here, regarding not making your fasting obvious, is that it is never meant to be a public display of spirituality. It is between you and God alone.

We must never view fasting as a way of pressuring God to get what we want. Fasting is not a way to earn God's favour by getting Him to do something for us, God's love is unconditional. As with all spiritual patterns it's not about earning God's love, as we already have that, it's about us loving Him and knowing Him more.

The purpose is to produce a transformation in us, a clearer, more focused attention and dependence upon God.

At a very practical level there are a few things you can do to prepare for a fast.

Know why you are fasting – it will help you prepare, study and pray more intentionally. Make your commitment. How long will you fast for, what are you fasting from, are there any physical or social activities you need to restrict, how much time will you devote each day to prayer and reading Scripture. Prepare spiritually. Begin with an expectant heart, but also be aware of the spiritual opposition you may come against. Prepare physically. Maybe eat smaller meals leading into your fast, decrease your caffeine and sugar intake, limit your exercise and have space to rest.

As followers of Jesus we are called to fast as part of our spiritual patterns which help us build intimacy and know Him more.

ACTION

Have you tried fasting before and what is your reflection on that?
Are there things in your life that you could deny for the sake of building a more intimate relationship with Jesus?
Can you build fasting into a regular spiritual discipline?

Seventeen

Store up treasures in heaven

Key Reference: Matt. 6:19-24
Other References: Luke 16:1-13

NLT

"Don't store up treasures here on earth, where moths eat them and rust destroys them, and where thieves break in and steal. Store your treasures in heaven, where moths and rust cannot destroy, and thieves do not break in and steal. Wherever your treasure is, there the desires of your heart will also be. "Your eye is a lamp that provides light for your body. When your eye is good, your whole body is filled with light. But when your eye is bad, your whole body is filled with darkness. And if the light you think you have is actually darkness, how deep that darkness is! "No one can serve two masters. For you will hate one and love the other; you will be devoted to one and despise the other. You cannot serve both God and money."

MSG

"Don't hoard treasure down here where it gets eaten by moths and corroded by rust or - worse! - stolen by burglars. Stockpile treasure in heaven, where it's safe from moth and rust and burglars. It's obvious, isn't it? The place where your treasure is, is the place you will most want to be, and end up being. "Your eyes are windows into your body. If you open your eyes wide in wonder and belief, your body fills up with light. If you live squinty-eyed in greed and distrust, your body is a dank cellar. If you pull the blinds on your windows, what a dark life you will have! "You can't worship two gods at once. Loving one god, you'll end up hating the other. Adoration of one feeds contempt for the other. You can't worship God and Money both."

After love, money is the second most talked about topic in the Bible. However, when Jesus says, "you cannot serve both God and money", money is not the best translation, as the original word used is mammon.

Mammon is an Aramaic word that refers to the desire to pursue wealth as a primary goal. Money of itself is not bad and when you think about it, it has no power. Money is just something we have created to trade, but mammon is a spirit and it can have power.

Any spirit, like mammon, that is not of God is about controlling your heart and your loyalty. Mammon fights to be the priority in your life. It's seeking to take the place of God in your life.

As a spirit, mammon wants our time and our allegiance. We are constantly fighting whether we give our allegiance to the supply (the asset or material thing) or to the supplier (God).

If we don't have worldly wealth, mammon makes us think it will fix things, so in this sense more money gives us status, power and control. If we do have worldly wealth, then mammon tells us that we have control or that we always need more.

In either case, you can see the issue with mammon that Jesus is talking about and why you have to choose between serving it or God.

What He encourages us to do is to think about building our riches in heaven, not here on earth.

In my family, we've had times of nothing and we've also had times of abundance. What we have learnt through these seasons is that neither is correlated to whether we've been closer or further from God. We've not been more or less blessed by God on earth, relative to our proximity to Him. The real answer is about being obedient to what God calls you to do with the resources He has put in your hands to steward, regardless of the amount.

So the question becomes, what to do about mammon in your life?

The first is to look at whether you have let mammon slip into your life. Keep in mind that mammon blinds you as to whether you are living with mammon, so you need to take an honest review. Consider some of these questions to help:
- do you have anxiety over unmet needs?
- do you have fear about your financial future?
- are you living with an attitude of a consumer or a steward?
- are you living beyond your means?
- are you giving part of your money as an offering to God in some way?

If you find you have mammon in your life then repent, turn away from that way of life (you can revisit command four to help with this). Finally, the best way to overcome mammon is to generously give, because giving is one of the most tangible ways we can worship God.

ACTION
What can you do to store up treasures in heaven?
How do you worship God with your finances and wealth?
How can you orient your heart towards an attitude of giving?

Eighteen
Seek first the kingdom of God

Key Reference: Matt. 6:25-34
Other References: Luke 12:22-34

NLT

"So don't worry about these things, saying, 'What will we eat? What will we drink? What will we wear?' These things dominate the thoughts of unbelievers, but your heavenly Father already knows all your needs. Seek the Kingdom of God above all else, and live righteously, and He will give you everything you need. So don't worry about tomorrow, for tomorrow will bring its own worries. Today's trouble is enough for today."

MSG

"What I'm trying to do here is to get you to relax, to not be so preoccupied with getting, so you can respond to God's giving. People who don't know God and the way He works fuss over these things, but you know both God and how He works. Steep your life in God-reality, God-initiative, God-provisions. Don't worry about missing out. You'll find all your everyday human concerns will be met. Give your entire attention to what God is doing right now, and don't get worked up about what may or may not happen tomorrow. God will help you deal with whatever hard things come up when the time comes."

This is one my favourite things that Jesus said and I find helps put so much of life into perspective.

To understand how we seek first the Kingdom of God, we need to understand what the concept of a kingdom is. A kingdom is defined as the domain a king rules over. The king is king over those who submit, and although that sounds simple, there are some issues with that.

It is hard for us to grasp the concept of a kingdom because we live in a democratic society. We are not used to serving in a kingdom, following the will of the king, because we are more about our own rights. Democracy was not a concept birthed by God and originally came from Greek philosophers.

Our rights have become an important part of our society and while there are many positives to this, it creates generations of people who are self-entitled. We can care about our own welfare over the needs of others and over the plans and purposes of God.

This is running in parallel to our desire of instant gratification, where we want what we want, when we want it. We can also be who we want to be, and that creates a status of individualism. All of this goes in the face of the concept of kingdom.

People in our society don't really live in submission to a king, but rather live as the king over their own life. We can desire the things of the king and not the will of the king. In complete contrast to this, so much of what Jesus spoke about was the Kingdom of God. There is so much we can explore as to what the Kingdom of God is and how we live as a Kingdom citizen while we physically live of earth. Many of the commands of Jesus in this devotional are really teaching us Kingdom living.

For now, let's focus on what Jesus was saying in this command – seek first.

No matter what issue, challenge or question in life you have, no matter what dream or ambition you are pursuing, or decision you need to make, I believe the answer is this: "Seek first the Kingdom of God". One way you can use this to help is to use the word FIRST as an acronym for Finances, Interests, Relationships, Schedule, Troubles. In other words:

Finances: If you have to make a decision about finances – how does it honour God, how does it keep Him first, does it echo His way of generosity?

Interests: Our interests are those things that allow us to disconnect from the everyday pressures of life. Our interests are not time out from God – but time with God.

Relationships: Think about the people who speak into your life, the balance you have between Christian and Non-Christian friends, those people who are building into you, the challenging people you are choosing to love, the people that you wrongly idolise.

Schedule: Time is something we all get to choose what we do with. Ultimately where you spend your time is the choice of what you are most passionate about. How does that align to what God calls you to do? How do you follow His rhythm of work and rest?

Troubles: When there are challenges in your life, where do you turn first? Do you rely on your own strength to solve the problem or seek God and try to understand what He is doing in the situation? Do you believe He is always involved and trust His sovereignty?

Seek first the kingdom of God.

ACTION

Can you identify how you live between a democracy and a kingdom?
Are there any changes you need to make to align to the principles we've explored with the "FIRST" acronym?
Are there any questions in your life that can now be answered by this?

Nineteen

Do not judge

Key Reference: Matt. 7:1-5
Other References: Luke 6:37

NLT

"Do not judge others, and you will not be judged. For you will be treated as you treat others. The standard you use in judging is the standard by which you will be judged. And why worry about a speck in your friend's eye when you have a log in your own? How can you think of saying to your friend, 'Let me help you get rid of that speck in your eye,' when you can't see past the log in your own eye? Hypocrite! First get rid of the log in your own eye; then you will see well enough to deal with the speck in your friend's eye."

MSG

"Don't pick on people, jump on their failures, criticize their faults - unless, of course, you want the same treatment. That critical spirit has a way of boomeranging. It's easy to see a smudge on your neighbour's face and be oblivious to the ugly sneer on your own. Do you have the nerve to say, 'Let me wash your face for you,' when your own face is distorted by contempt? It's this whole traveling road-show mentality all over again, playing a holier-than-thou part instead of just living your part. Wipe that ugly sneer off your own face, and you might be fit to offer a washcloth to your neighbour."

This command makes it explicit that it is not our role to judge, but God's. I don't know about you, but it seems there are many people who have left churches because they have felt judged. The truth is though, that this is not a church thing, but a human heart condition.

Judgement is different to the situations where we are meant to hold people to account. Consider when Jesus says in Matthew (Matt. 18:15-17): "If another believer sins against you, go and privately point out the offense", or where Paul says to the Corinthians (1 Cor. 5:12): "It isn't my responsibility to judge outsiders, but it certainly is your responsibility to judge those inside the church who are sinning".

It's in examples like these that we need to make sure we never build a theology around single lines of Scripture. Our theology needs to be built on a holistic view of Scripture. Here we see that accountability to support other Christians in their journey is important, to call out sin to help each other chase after righteousness. But that is not then meant to lead to judgement, making assumptions about that person, or treating them differently.

So, to put this command into practice, let's consider a couple of points. We are to look inwards first, to consider our own actions and behaviours. Right relationships with one another are dependent on a right relationship with God, so we need to have our own regular check-ups. David spoke on this well in the Psalms when He said, "Search me, O God, and know my heart; test me and know my anxious thoughts. Point out anything in me that offends you, and lead me along the path of everlasting life." (Psalm 139:23-24).

Jesus' analogy here is great where He says take care of the log in your eye before you look to remove the speck in someone else's. In other words, to clearly see the speck in someone else, to be able to approach their speck in love, we need to start with our own issues. As we looked at before, holding one another to account, but not judging is an important part of the Christian journey. Jesus doesn't say here not to remove the speck in someone else's eye, but to make sure we have removed our own log first.

To not judge is to avoid external evaluations of others. To give people the benefit of the doubt. To do that you often have to catch your thoughts. We easily start making assumptions about people and we have to learn a behaviour that avoids this and assumes the best. Remember, you never know what is going on behind the scenes for people. Learn to live in a state where you approach life with a cool head and a warm heart. When Jesus talks about loving people, this issue of judgement is one of those "rubber hits the road" moments.

If you feel you have been judging someone, now's a great opportunity to seek forgiveness from Jesus and possibly from them directly. Also, if you feel you have been unfairly judged and may be wearing labels from that which are impacting the way you live, you need to be released from that and walk in the freedom and identity that you have in Jesus.

ACTION
Can you change your thought patterns of people from judgement to assuming the best?
Is there anyone that you know you regularly judge, that you need to seek forgiveness from?
Do you need to walk in the freedom and identity of Christ from times you have been judged?

Twenty

Do not throw your pearls to pigs

Key Reference: Matt. 7:6

NLT

"Do not give dogs what is sacred. Don't throw your pearls to pigs! They will trample the pearls, then turn and attack you."

MSG

"Don't be flip with the sacred. Banter and silliness give no honour to God. Don't reduce holy mysteries to slogans. In trying to be relevant, you're only being cute and inviting sacrilege."

To understand what Jesus is referring to we need to get a context of pigs and dogs in Jesus' time. Pigs are not dissimilar to what probably comes to mind when you think of pigs today, they are depicted as unclean and dirty. Back in the Law of Moses, all Israelites were to keep their distance from swine.

Like the pigs, dogs were also seen as demeaning in Biblical times. Unlike today where they are domesticated and seen as man's best friend, in Jesus time they were also seen as unclean, as there used to be packs of wild dogs that would feed on the dead. They were associated with mockery and insult and used to refer to the wrongdoers of society.

This is contrasted by the use of the word "pearls", which is symbolic of godly wisdom and the salvation brought by His kingdom. The pearl is also used in one of Jesus' other parables where He is likening it to the Kingdom of Heaven (Matt. 13:44-46).

Jesus is using the analogy of dogs and pigs as representative of those who would ridicule, reject and blaspheme the Gospel once it is presented to them. Once we have presented the Gospel, if it is clear that it is not welcome, or someone has no purpose but to return to their evil ways, then we are to move on.

This doesn't mean that we refrain from sharing the Gospel all together.

We know that Jesus spent a lot of His time with sinners, but we see Him live this out practically where He said to His disciples as He sent them out, "If any household or town refuses to welcome you or listen to your message, shake its dust from your feet as you leave." (Matt. 10:14).

This same context is echoed by Peter. He says, "And when people escape from the wickedness of the world by knowing our Lord and Saviour Jesus Christ and then get tangled up and enslaved by sin again, they are worse off than before. It would be better if they had never known the way to righteousness than to know it and then reject the command they were given to live a holy life." (2 Pet. 2:20-21).

He goes on to make the connection with dogs and pigs, "They prove the truth of this proverb: "A dog returns to its vomit (Prov. 26:11)." And another says, "A washed pig returns to the mud." (2 Pet. 2:22).

We need to reconcile this with the times Jesus says to chase after people with the Gospel. For example, where He says to leave the ninety-nine sheep to go after the one lost sheep (Matt. 18:12-14). The way we do this is by listening to Him and getting discernment for the situation (1 Cor. 2:15). We are responsible to share the Gospel, but we are not responsible for people's response to the Gospel.

Pigs don't appreciate pearls and some people do not appreciate what Jesus has done for them. Jesus instructs us not to force the issue and the way that we handle the rejection is to simply go elsewhere. There are other people who need to hear the Gospel and are ready to hear it.

ACTION
Are you sharing the Gospel regularly?
Have you had a time where it is clear someone does not want to listen or accept what you are saying?
Can you find discernment to know when to pursue someone with the Gospel versus moving on?

Twenty One
Ask, seek and knock

Key Reference: Matt. 7:7-11
Other References: Luke 11:9-10

NLT

"Keep on asking, and you will receive what you ask for. Keep on seeking, and you will find. Keep on knocking, and the door will be opened to you. For everyone who asks, receives. Everyone who seeks, finds. And to everyone who knocks, the door will be opened. You parents - if your children ask for a loaf of bread, do you give them a stone instead? Or if they ask for a fish, do you give them a snake? Of course not! So if you sinful people know how to give good gifts to your children, how much more will your heavenly Father give good gifts to those who ask him."

MSG

"Don't bargain with God. Be direct. Ask for what you need. This isn't a cat-and-mouse, hide-and-seek game we're in. If your child asks for bread, do you trick him with sawdust? If He asks for fish, do you scare him with a live snake on His plate? As bad as you are, you wouldn't think of such a thing. You're at least decent to your own children. So don't you think the God who conceived you in love will be even better?"

Jesus is talking about prayer again in this command and our interactions with Him. He is giving us permission to ask for the things that we desire, to seek out the things we wish to have in our life and to knock to get His attention concerning the things we need.

Jesus is not saying that we always get what we ask for and we need to keep our motives fixed on His kingdom. We have seen this in a previous command of Jesus: "Seek first His kingdom and all these things will be added unto you" (Matt. 6:25-34), but James also echoes this when He says, "Yet you don't have what you want because you don't ask God for it. And even when you ask, you don't get it because your motives are all wrong—you want only what will give you pleasure" (James 4:2-3).

The more time we spend with God, the more we know what to ask for in accordance with His will. In this command, there are three different ways Jesus encourages us to pray.

Asking is verbal. We speak out to petition God for our needs and desires. It's not that He is unaware of our needs as He knows what we need before we ask Him (Matt. 6:8), but just as we talk over our issues with our family and friends, God wants us to communicate with Him about the issues and needs that are on our mind.

Seeking then is about setting our priorities and focus on His heart. We need to look around to see how God may answer our prayers. We need to have eyes of faith to believe how God may provide answers for the issues we have shared with Him.

The final step then is knocking. This is the physical move where we take action. It's like when John says we can't love in word alone but need actions also (1 John 3:18). It's about stepping out in faith, in response to what we have perceived when we seek the answers to the prayers we have asked for. It's not always the first door that we knock on that opens and perseverance is important sometimes to see answers to our prayers.

The commands on how to pray are followed by promises. Everyone who asks receives, if you seek you find and if you knock the door will be opened. God delights in our prayers of faith and promises to give us what we need, when it is aligned to His kingdom will.

ACTION
When you pray, do you pray in faith believing God will hear and answer your prayers?
How can you mix the prayer of words with the physical action of knocking, when you are asking God to help with your requests?

Twenty Two

Do unto others as you would have them do to you

Key Reference: Matt. 7:12

NLT

*"Do to others whatever you would like them to do to you.
This is the essence of all that is taught in the law and the prophets."*

MSG

*"Here is a simple, rule-of-thumb guide for behavior: Ask yourself what you want
people to do for you, then grab the initiative and do it for them. Add up God's Law
and Prophets and this is what you get."*

This command by Jesus is often referred to as "The Golden Rule" and a version of it appears in many other religious writings. Confucius said, "Never impose on others what you would not choose for yourself". In the Hindu religion, it says "One should never do that to another which one regards as injurious to one's own self".

On a closer look, some of these are written as a positive and the others as a negative and this is part of why Christianity is different. They basically say don't do to others what you don't want done to yourself. This is about inaction and self-protection – using the words "Don't do".

What Jesus says is about His action. We love others as a response because God first loved us, and our response is part of our worship.

So how do we do unto others? There are some great Scriptures that talk about this. Consider Isaiah's writings, "Is not this the kind of fasting I have chosen: to loose the chains of injustice and untie the cords of the yoke, to set the oppressed free and break every yoke? Is it not to share your food with the hungry and to provide the poor wanderer with shelter - when you see the naked, to clothe them?" (Isa. 58:6-7).

Or in Matthew where Jesus says, "They also will answer, 'Lord, when did we see you hungry or thirsty or a stranger or needing clothes or sick or in prison, and did not help you?' He will reply, 'Truly I tell you, whatever you did not do for one of the least of these, you did not do for me.'" (Matt. 2:44-45).

This is about practical love – showing others love as a way of demonstrating God's love to them, and this comes up in Jesus' other commands. But it's not just about the practical love of charity.

We do unto others by sharing the Gospel with them. To care for people is to want to see them in relationship with Jesus. You are a smart person and have made a decision to follow Jesus – so why wouldn't you want to tell others to do the same.

The final way we can do unto others is the spiritual aspect – to bring the power of God into their lives. Paul says the kingdom of God is not a matter of talk but of power (1 Cor. 4:20). If you were sick and someone could pray for you, wouldn't you want that? If you needed wisdom or discernment and someone could pray for you to help with that, wouldn't you want that? It's about having the boldness to trust the power of the Holy Spirit within you and spiritually love people.

ACTION

How would you like other people to treat you?

How do you transform this into a way of life regarding how you treat other people?

What are some ways you can love other people, either through practical love, sharing the Gospel or bringing the power of God into a situation?

Twenty Three
Choose the narrow road

Key Reference: Matt. 7:13-14
Other References: Luke 13:23-30

NLT

"You can enter God's Kingdom only through the narrow gate. The highway to hell is broad, and its gate is wide for the many who choose that way. But the gateway to life is very narrow and the road is difficult, and only a few ever find it."

MSG

"Don't look for shortcuts to God. The market is flooded with surefire, easygoing formulas for a successful life that can be practiced in your spare time. Don't fall for that stuff, even though crowds of people do. The way to life - to God! - is vigorous and requires total attention."

The analogy of the narrow gate versus the wide gate is relatively simple to understand. A narrow gate is harder to pass through than one that is wide, and only a few people can go through a narrow gate at once. In saying "difficult is the way which leads to life", Jesus was explaining how hard being a Christian really is. To clarify – Jesus is the gate or door through which every person must enter for eternal life. John says that Jesus is "the way, and the truth, and the life." (John 14:6). Eternal life comes by whether a person believes in Jesus, entering through Him as the gate.

On the one hand, salvation is not hard to find. It is not based on our works, but on faith and belief in Jesus. Paul wrote in Ephesians: "God saved you by His grace when you believed. And you can't take credit for this; it is a gift from God. Salvation is not a reward for the good things we have done, so none of us can boast about it." (Eph. 2:8-9).

However, because salvation in Jesus requires choosing Him as Lord of your life, there is a commitment involved that requires repentance of sin and a turn toward living by His ways. Even though it is a "free" gift of eternal life, many refuse to accept it, and instead choose the "wide gate" that seems easier at the time, yet leads to destruction.

As a follower of Jesus, sometimes it's hard to understand why people don't see the amazing life you get to live with Jesus, but if you think about it, even when Jesus himself walked on earth, there were more people that rejected Him, than accepted Him. For all the people Jesus ministered to, and the thousands that were often in His presence, there were only a few hundred left as His followers after His death (see Acts 1:15 and 1 Cor. 15:6).

When you read from this perspective in the Gospels there are three clear occasions where someone was presented with the Gospel, but chose the "wide gate". One of them made the statement of commitment, saying to Jesus: "Lord, I will follow You wherever You go" (Luke 9:57-62). Jesus articulated the reality of this "Foxes have holes and birds of the air have nests, but the Son of Man has nowhere to lay His head".

He then asks another person to follow Him and the man asks to be allowed to first bury His father. Jesus responded saying: "Let the dead bury their own dead, but you go and preach the kingdom of God". Jesus was referring to those who were spiritually dead - people who had not responded to His teaching and He is telling the person He was speaking to that His calling was more important.

Then a third person who wanted to become a disciple, made a request to first return home to say goodbye to whoever was at His house. Jesus responded: "No one, having put His hand to the plough, and looking back, is fit for the kingdom of God".

It is clear from what Jesus is saying that His way is the narrow way, but the reward - to do the journey of life with your creator and have eternal relationship with Him – is worth it.

ACTION
What parts of the road do you find "narrow"?
Do you believe that for the challenges of the Christian life it is worth persevering?
How might you present this message to someone who isn't yet a Christian?

Twenty Four
Beware of false prophets

Key Reference: Matt. 7:15-19
Other References: Luke 6:43-45

NLT

"Beware of false prophets who come disguised as harmless sheep but are really vicious wolves. You can identify them by their fruit, that is, by the way they act. Can you pick grapes from thornbushes, or figs from thistles? A good tree produces good fruit, and a bad tree produces bad fruit. A good tree can't produce bad fruit, and a bad tree can't produce good fruit. So every tree that does not produce good fruit is chopped down and thrown into the fire. Yes, just as you can identify a tree by its fruit, so you can identify people by their actions."

MSG

Be wary of false preachers who smile a lot, dripping with practiced sincerity. Chances are they are out to rip you off some way or other. Don't be impressed with charisma; look for character. Who preachers are is the main thing, not what they say. A genuine leader will never exploit your emotions or your pocketbook. These diseased trees with their bad apples are going to be chopped down and burned."

This command of Jesus is about who you follow and who follows you. Jesus cautions us to be aware of who or what we are following. We might think it seems strange to follow a teaching that's not right – but humanity has been following many false teachings over time. Consider some of these things that people have believed that turned out not to be true:

- The world is flat (Columbus 1492)
- The universe centred around the earth (Copernicus, 1543)
- A rocket will never be able to leave earth (New York Times, 1920)
- The cinema is just a fad, people will want to see flesh and blood on stage (Charlie Chaplin, 1916)
- The world's potential for copying machines is 5,000 (IBM, 1959)
- Don't invest in Ford, the horse is here to stay (Michigan Savings Bank, 1903)

These might seem humorous now, but were thoughts seriously followed at the time. It shows how simply, but subtly, we can find ourselves following false teaching. This can also be true of spiritual doctrine. We need to be careful that we are following teaching that is completely consistent with a holistic view of Scripture. There is a lot of teaching we encounter in our world today where theology is built around single line Scriptures.

We also need to make sure that we listen to Jesus' teaching and Scripture as our primary source. With access to so much teaching from great preachers and teachers, through books and podcasts, it can be easy to make these our primary source, when they should be a secondary source.

The key message here is to be intentional about what teaching you listen to and in contrast, the truth of the teaching you give. Jesus lets us know that we can check for the right kind of teaching by the fruit in their life. Consider some of the people you listen to – what does the fruit in their life look like?

To examine the fruit in someone's life – consider the following aspects of fruit.

Something usually dies to produce fruit. The fruit of an apple isn't another apple – but another apple tree. When we let God deal with the stuff in our lives He wants to, things die, and when we let something die, it bears fruit.

Fruit isn't what you see in the short term. If you look at grape vines that have been irrigated, they produce fruit quicker, but they have skinnier branches and the fruit is watery.

This contrasts with fruit that is not irrigated where the roots need to go deeper. It takes longer to produce fruit, but it develops a trunk and root system that is stronger, and the fruit is far richer and sweeter. People can wow you for a short time, but what does their life look like over a longer period.

Finally, look at Paul's list of the fruits of the Spirit and determine whether these are evident in a teacher's life: love, joy, peace, patience, kindness, goodness, self-control (Gal. 5:22-23).

Remember, a good teacher will always bear good fruit in their life.

ACTION

What teachers do you intentionally listen to?

What does the fruit in their life look like over a long period of time?

How do you make sure that Jesus is your primary source of teaching?

Twenty Five

Do the will of the Father in heaven

Key Reference: Matt. 7:21-27
Other References: Luke 6:46-49

NLT

"Not everyone who calls out to me, 'Lord! Lord!' will enter the Kingdom of Heaven. Only those who actually do the will of my Father in heaven will enter. On judgment day many will say to me, 'Lord! Lord! We prophesied in your name and cast out demons in your name and performed many miracles in your name.' But I will reply, 'I never knew you. Get away from me, you who break God's laws.' Anyone who listens to my teaching and follows it is wise, like a person who builds a house on solid rock. Though the rain comes in torrents and the floodwaters rise and the winds beat against that house, it won't collapse because it is built on bedrock. But anyone who hears my teaching and doesn't obey it is foolish, like a person who builds a house on sand. When the rains and floods come and the winds beat against that house, it will collapse with a mighty crash."

MSG

"Knowing the correct password—saying 'Master, Master,' for instance—isn't going to get you anywhere with me. What is required is serious obedience—doing what my Father wills. I can see it now—at the Final Judgment thousands strutting up to me and saying, 'Master, we preached the Message, we bashed the demons, our God-sponsored projects had everyone talking.' And do you know what I am going to say? 'You missed the boat. All you did was use me to make yourselves important. You're out of here.' These words I speak to you are not incidental additions to your life, homeowner improvements to your standard of living. They are foundational words, words to build a life on.

The thought of this command might be confronting, did I do the will of God and will I be accepted into heaven?

We do need to be compelled towards the will of God, but the fact that you are working through this devotional book shows that you are seeking His will and putting it into action. Jesus tells us that anyone who listens to His teaching and follows it, is building on a strong foundation.

Our lives are built on all sorts of foundations.

As a Christian, it's our theology and worldview that shape the decisions that we make. At the start of our journey this is reset, as Paul wrote, "This means that anyone who belongs to Christ has become a new person. The old life is gone; a new life has begun" (2 Cor. 5:17). To do the will of the Father is to continue to build from this foundation and to continue to become more like Jesus.

This is a constant renewing that Paul refers to in Colossians, "Put on your new nature, and be renewed as you learn to know your Creator and become like him." (Col. 3:10).

This concept of a solid foundation is echoed throughout Scripture. Consider the Psalm, "The Lord is my rock, my fortress, and my saviour; my God is my rock, in whom I find protection. He is my shield, the power that saves me, and my place of safety." (Psalm 18:2) and Corinthians, "For no one can lay any foundation other than the one we already have - Jesus Christ." (1 Cor. 3:11).

Jesus is our Rock – the firm foundation that we can build our lives upon. If we follow His teaching, He is assuring us that no matter what flood comes our way, how fierce the storms of life get, that we will never fall or be destroyed.

He says that we are to come to Him, listen to His teaching and to then follow it. Notice how it is not just about hearing the teaching, it is about following it. This is why I wrote this book and include actions after each chapter, to find ways to help us put the teachings immediately into practice.

James says, "But don't just listen to God's word. You must do what it says. Otherwise, you are only fooling yourselves." (James 1:22).

We come to Jesus as the King, our Lord and Saviour. We listen to hear what He says as the truth. We follow, put it into action and live a life of obedience.

We can hear the truth, but does it mean that we will always obey?

As we have mentioned, obeying is not just a religious act of mindlessly following a set of rules. Paul says that "God saved you by His grace when you believed. And you can't take credit for this; it is a gift from God. Salvation is not a reward for the good things we have done, so none of us can boast about it." (Eph. 2:8-9). Obeying is not about earning our salvation, this is what Jesus has done, but it is about our worship and our response to what Jesus has done for us.

ACTION
What foundations have you built your life upon?
How are these actions rather than just words?
What does it mean to have Jesus as your rock and your refuge?

Twenty Six

Preach the kingdom of God, heal the sick and cast out demons

Key Reference: Luke 9:1-5
Other References: Matt. 10:6-7

NLT

One day Jesus called together His twelve disciples and gave them power and authority to cast out all demons and to heal all diseases. Then He sent them out to tell everyone about the Kingdom of God and to heal the sick. ³ "Take nothing for your journey," He instructed them. "Don't take a walking stick, a traveler's bag, food, money, or even a change of clothes. Wherever you go, stay in the same house until you leave town. And if a town refuses to welcome you, shake its dust from your feet as you leave to show that you have abandoned those people to their fate."

MSG

Jesus now called the Twelve and gave them authority and power to deal with all the demons and cure diseases. He commissioned them to preach the news of God's kingdom and heal the sick. He said, "Don't load yourselves up with equipment. Keep it simple; you are the equipment. And no luxury inns - get a modest place and be content there until you leave. If you're not welcomed, leave town. Don't make a scene. Shrug your shoulders and move on."

A lot of the commands of Jesus we have looked at so far came out of what is known as His Sermon on the Mount. He'd spent that time teaching His disciples, preaching and healing the sick around Galilee. Now He is giving His disciples their first mission – to preach the Kingdom, heal the sick and cast out demons.

He gave the same mission to the seventy followers in Luke 10 – and it is the same mission for us today.

This mission is about proclamation and demonstration. Proclamation is sharing and speaking the Gospel. Demonstration is sharing the love of God in a practical way and allowing God to work through you to see His supernatural power at work.

There are two recent studies on Christians sharing the Gospel. One says that only 1 in 20 Christians have ever shared the Gospel – the other says 61% of Christians have never shared the Gospel. Either way – the numbers demonstrate is it more unlikely that you have shared the Gospel. Hopefully that's not you. Sharing the Gospel is a fundamental part of being a Christian. As a follower of Jesus, you have discovered the truth so why wouldn't you want to share that with others that you care about?

If we consider the reasons, maybe it is that we don't know how, maybe we are embarrassed or maybe it is just complacency. If you relate to any of those, I pray that you see people as God sees them, and have an urgency to see their salvation, which may compel you towards sharing the Good News of Jesus with them.

With this step of proclamation, it is about using words. If you don't know how to share the basics of the Gospel message, then it's important to take some time to get it in your own words in a way that you can share over a couple of minutes. You can also look in Scripture at how Peter (Acts 2:16-41) or Paul (Acts 17:16-31) shared the Gospel.

The other perspective on sharing the Gospel, is sharing your story. Peter says, "Instead, you must worship Christ as Lord of your life. And if someone asks about your hope as a believer, always be ready to explain it." (1 Pet. 3:15). Your story is part of the ongoing story of the Gospel. Learn how to describe what your life was like before becoming a Christian, the encounter you had with Jesus that made you choose to follow Him, and what life is like now. This is your version of the Gospel message.

Demonstration, as Jesus says, is to heal the sick and cast out demons. It is to show the manifest power of God. Paul says, "For the kingdom of God is not a matter of talk but of power." (1 Cor. 4:20). One of the easiest ways to do this is to have the courage to ask someone if you can pray for them. If they are sharing challenges of life with you, then what a great opportunity to see the power of God demonstrated in their life. The Spirit of God is within you and He works through us in a spiritual way to bring healing, cast out demons, bring words of knowledge, the prophetic and more. Our role is to be obedient with this and then let God choose how He answers the prayer.

ACTION
Have you ever had the chance to share the Gospel?
If you had to share the Gospel in just a few minutes what would you say?
Are you prepared to pray for someone next time they are sharing an issue with you?

Twenty Seven

Be as shrewd as snakes and innocent as doves

Key Reference: Matt. 10:16

NLT
*"Look, I am sending you out as sheep among wolves.
So be as shrewd as snakes and harmless as doves"*

MSG
"Stay alert. This is hazardous work I'm assigning you. You're going to be like sheep running through a wolf pack, so don't call attention to yourselves. Be as cunning as a snake, inoffensive as a dove."

Jesus has just sent out His twelve disciples with instructions to go into the homes of Israelites proclaiming the kingdom of heaven, healing the sick and driving out demons. It is with this context He gives what is the strange command to be shrewd as snakes and innocent as doves.

The choice of a snake is an interesting analogy given the other references to snakes or serpents in the Bible. The most obvious ones being the snake representing the devil in the creation story (Gen. 3:1), as well as in the book of Revelation (Rev. 12:9). With many symbols, they can have both a positive and negative meaning and the ancient Hebrews also viewed the snake as a symbol of wisdom.

The original word shrewd, in this context, is understood as cunning or wise. Therefore, we can think about what Jesus was saying in the sense of being prepared – think ahead and anticipate what might happen. To be cautious and practice discernment. This analogy is then balanced by being as innocent as doves. Doves were among the list of clean animals used for sacrifice as an offering for cleanliness (Lev. 14:22). Still to this day doves are used as a symbol of peace. This symbolism teaches us to live a pure and holy life. To keep a good conscience before God. To show compassion and mercy.

Jesus pre-empts this command by stating that He is sending out His disciples as sheep among the wolves. Our Christian walk is about going into the world with the Kingdom message. In many of these situations we will have opposition and Jesus is giving us some general principles of the technique for this Kingdom work.

We can find examples of this in Paul's life. In some circumstances, such as Acts

23:1, He lived innocently and in good conscience before God. In other situations, He displayed shrewdness, knowing His legal rights and using the system to His advantage (see Acts 22:25 for one example).

Notice that Jesus has sent His disciples out amongst the wolves. In other words, our Christian journey is not meant to be lived within our comfort zone. We are to be in the world spreading the Kingdom message. We need to find that place in between our comfort zone and the danger zone – the place I call the God zone. This is the sweet spot God wants us to be in, the faith zone, the miracle zone, the breakthrough zone. Where in your life right now do you need faith in God? If there's nothing coming to mind, perhaps you are living in your comfort zone.

In the God zone – there's no better way to grow. Each step forward makes it easier to take the next step forward, as you gain confidence and experience – you are always learning. If you get in the God zone, you'll find new opportunities that were previously obscured by the boundaries of your comfort zone.

As a Christian, this command of Jesus can help us in our decision making. The shrewdness means that we can make careful plans, be strategic and commercial in our approach, but the harmlessness means that we are honest, transparent and show compassion for people. Finding the balance between these is a good lesson to learn.

ACTION

Are you living in your God zone – the place between your comfort zone and your danger zone?
Do you need to change some behaviours to be living more innocently or shrewdly?

Twenty Eight
Fear only God

Key Reference: Matt. 10:28

Other References: Luke 12:4-5

NLT
"Don't be afraid of those who want to kill your body; they cannot touch your soul. Fear only God, who can destroy both soul and body in hell."

MSG
"Don't be bluffed into silence by the threats of bullies. There's nothing they can do to your soul, your core being. Save your fear for God, who holds your entire life - body and soul - in His hands."

Fear means the unpleasant emotion that is caused by the threat of danger, pain or harm. In this command, Jesus is addressing the difference between fear of God (which can be a healthy fear) and fear of man, meaning other humans (which is an unhealthy fear).

A fear of God is a healthy thing. It is about recognizing our creator is Almighty. It's about having reverence and not forgetting who God is. By recognising that He is more powerful than any human – it builds confidence in our faith to know that He will help and protect us.

The result of this fear is security, hope and joy. Proverbs says that "the fear of the Lord is the beginning of wisdom." (Prov. 9:10).

Many of the unpleasant feelings we have – anxiety, worry and feeling down can be traced back to the unhealthy fear of man. I remember several years ago I had a situation where I was facing extreme stress and anxiety in relation to a business matter. A party had invested in our business and having spent the money on a growth strategy, it wasn't working, and it looked like we were going to have to lay off staff, maybe close the business and lose the investor's money. While that was an unpleasant situation, my wife helped me reflect on where the stress and anxiety was coming from.

The first part of that was realising that those feelings were based in fear.

Fear often takes our mind to places that are far worse than what reality is likely to look like. In my case, if I did lose the business, which felt catastrophic, it didn't mean I lost my faith, or my family, and I was young enough to rebuild. From there I could reflect on where the fear was coming from. This was a fear of failure and a fear of man – in other words if I did fail, I was most concerned of what people were going to think of me.

These types of fears can immobilize you - impacting the way you think and your habits. It feels like it has power over your life, but it is just deceiving you into a wrong pattern of thinking. It undermines your faith and can take you away from believing in the promises of God.

In my case – I had to learn to be more interested in what God thinks of me rather than people. If the circumstances of the business situation caused me to fear failure, I should look to Jesus to either help bring breakthrough or trust that either way, He still had me. I needed to believe some of the many promises we read in the Bible like "He will never leave me or forsake me." (Heb. 13:5).

Working through this situation brought an interesting revelation – that this type of fear is actually sin. It is a behaviour that is separating me from God and something that we need to repent from.

There are over one hundred references in the Bible to "fear not." Here's a couple of examples:

"For I am the Lord your God who takes hold of your right hand and says to you, do not fear I will help you." (Isa. 41:13).

"For the Spirit God gave us does not make us timid, but gives us power, love and self-discipline." (2 Tim. 1:7).

Because we have this unhealthy fear, it creates in us a fear of fear. This can make it difficult to experience the healthy fear of God. In this command Jesus is teaching us to transfer our fear to the right place. He helps us face our false fears, so that they lose their power over us.

ACTION
Are there some behaviours in your life that you can look at, that might be coming from an unhealthy fear?
Are you able to recognise them as sin and go to Jesus for repentance?
Is there anything you need to change in your life to have a healthy fear of the Lord?

Twenty Nine

Give up your life for Jesus

Key Reference: Luke 14:26-33

Other References: Matt. 10:34-40

NLT

"If you want to be my disciple, you must hate everyone else by comparison—your father and mother, wife and children, brothers and sisters—yes, even your own life. Otherwise, you cannot be my disciple. And if you do not carry your own cross and follow me, you cannot be my disciple. But don't begin until you count the cost. For who would begin construction of a building without first calculating the cost to see if there is enough money to finish it? Otherwise, you might complete only the foundation before running out of money, and then everyone would laugh at you. They would say, 'There's the person who started that building and couldn't afford to finish it!' Or what king would go to war against another king without first sitting down with His counselors to discuss whether His army of 10,000 could defeat the 20,000 soldiers marching against him? And if He can't, He will send a delegation to discuss terms of peace while the enemy is still far away. So you cannot become my disciple without giving up everything you own."

MSG

Anyone who comes to me but refuses to let go of father, mother, spouse, children, brothers, sisters - yes, even one's own self! - can't be my disciple. Anyone who won't shoulder His own cross and follow behind me can't be my disciple. Is there anyone here who, planning to build a new house, doesn't first sit down and figure the cost so you'll know if you can complete it? If you only get the foundation laid and then run out of money, you're going to look pretty foolish. Everyone passing by will poke fun at you: 'He started something He couldn't finish.' Or can you imagine a king going into battle against another king without first deciding whether it is possible with His ten thousand troops to face the twenty thousand troops of the other? And if He decides He can't, won't He send an emissary and work out a truce? Simply put, if you're not willing to take what is dearest to you, whether plans or people, and kiss it good-bye, you can't be my disciple."

At the outset of this command let's agree this is pretty heavy! Jesus is saying that to be His follower you must love him more than the people you love most in your life. You must be prepared to give up everything to be His disciple.

This is a recurring theme in Jesus' commands. It is similar to what we looked at with the third command "Worship God only" and it comes up again when we get to number thirty-five, "Deny yourself". Suffice to say, this is a message that Jesus really needed to get through to us and it makes sense because in our lives there are so many things that compete for our attention and distract us from what it really means to be a follower of Jesus.

When my wife and I felt called into ministry as Pastors it was included in our calling to sell our house and our car. It was an interesting test of where our loyalties lay, because we had worked hard overseas for several years and the location we were living in and the car we were driving, were things we had dreamed about for a long time. However our calling was so strong that it was an easy decision to give these things up, and it really released something in us when we truly submitted everything to God.

I'm not saying that you physically need to go and sell all your possessions, but it is an interesting test to see if there is anything in this world you are holding onto too tightly, that is preventing you from fully submitting your life to Jesus.

This is an issue of Lordship. We have already looked at the idea that as humans we all worship something, and this is what is Lord over our life. I've had times in my life when I have inappropriately allowed things to become a Lord in my life. I've mentioned possessions, but there are others like:

- Status: chasing job promotions or pay rises;
- Relationships: becoming over dependent on some key people in my life;
- Hobbies: spending too much time on improving skills in things that aren't important like my golf swing or surfing or guitar playing. Not that these things are bad, they are actually important as times of enjoyment or rest, but that can cross a line when they become obsessive.

I'm sharing some of these stories of my life as examples and hopefully they might help you recognise things that have become Lord in your life. The Bible says that Jesus is Lord of all and as James Hudson Taylor says: "unless Jesus is Lord of all – He is not Lord at all."

There are many things in this world competing for your worship, but when you make Jesus Lord of your life everything gets back in balance. Once the issue of Lordship is settled, it is like all the issues are settled: Your will not my will Lord; Lord of my speech; Lord of my emotions; Lord of my thoughts; Lord of my possessions, and the list goes on.

If there is anything in your life that is competing with Jesus as the main thing and wins, then you've got your Lordship in the wrong order. Remember, we are created to worship – so this isn't about trying to stop worshiping, but about turning back to Jesus to make sure He is Lord of our life.

ACTION

What things in your life right now do you think are competing to be your Lord?

What can you do now to reset and make sure that Jesus is the central Lord of your life?

Thirty

Listen to God's voice

Key Reference: Matt. 11:15

Other References: Matt. 13:9, Matt. 13:43, Mark 4:23, Luke 14:35

NLT

"Anyone with ears to hear should listen and understand!"

MSG

"Are you listening to me? Really listening?"

In relationships, we learn about each other through communication. Communication is two way where we learn to hear one another, to learn what each other's voice is like.

This is the same in our relationship with God. As a Pastor, I always think that one of the best things I can try and teach people is how to hear God.

There are many examples in the Bible of how people heard from God. You might have a favourite, but one I like is when God speaks to Elijah. He says to Elijah to go up to a mountain and be ready to hear Him. While he is there a windstorm came, then there was an earthquake and then there was fire. Now I would have thought that if God was going to speak – any one of those things might have been the way He was going to do it – but the Bible then says that God wasn't in any of those things – but after they had come, God spoke in a whisper. You see sometimes when God speaks – we have to listen carefully - it's not always in the obvious way we are expecting.

There are many things in our world that can drown out the voice of God, so we need to get in a place where we can hear the whisper, but if He is whispering, it is because He is close.

If I think back to the times I believe I've heard from God, it has often looked different. I have heard from God through creation, from other people, in my prayer times with him, through Scripture and through dreams.

Consider some of these Scriptures that reference how God speaks to us. Through Scripture: "All Scripture is inspired by God and is useful to teach us what is true and to make us realize what is wrong in our lives. It corrects us when we are wrong and teaches us to do what is right. God uses it to prepare and equip His people to do every good work." (2 Tim. 3:16-17).

Through your thoughts: "Don't copy the behaviour and customs of this world, but let God transform you into a new person by changing the way you think. Then you will learn to know God's will for you, which is good and pleasing and perfect." (Rom. 12:2).

Through dreams and visions: "In the last days' God says, 'I will pour out my Spirit upon all people. Your sons and daughters will prophesy. Your young men will see visions, and your old men will dream dreams." (Acts 2:17).

We need to begin with a belief that God will speak to us – this is what this command of Jesus is about. Often we feel like we can't hear from God, and it is then easy to assume that He is not speaking. Maybe consider what your expectation is of how God will speak. Perhaps He wants you to listen differently or is trying to teach you something.

Hearing is a choice, but we need to remember that responding to what we hear is also a choice. Jesus command here is that if we hear – we should listen and understand. We need to be prepared to do what it is that He is saying to us. In another part of the Gospels Jesus says, "But even more blessed are all who hear the word of God and put it into practice." (Luke 11:28).

Often we may hear God speaking through other people. To help you with this, bear in mind that any word someone gives you should be consistent with Scripture. It should bring life, freedom, mercy, grace and hope. It is also appropriate to take that word back to God yourself and test that it is from Him.

Paul wrote to the Thessalonians, "Do not stifle the Holy Spirit. Do not scoff at prophecies, but test everything that is said. Hold on to what is good." (1 Thess. 5:19-21).

ACTION
Reflect on the times that you feel God has spoken to you and how it happened?
Take some time now to stop and listen to what God may be saying to you.

Thirty One

Take Jesus' yoke and learn from him

Key Reference: Matt. 11:28-30

NLT

"Come to me, all of you who are weary and carry heavy burdens, and I will give you rest. Take my yoke upon you. Let me teach you, because I am humble and gentle at heart, and you will find rest for your souls. For my yoke is easy to bear, and the burden I give you is light."

MSG

Are you tired? Worn out? Burned out on religion? Come to me. Get away with me and you'll recover your life. I'll show you how to take a real rest. Walk with me and work with me - watch how I do it. Learn the unforced rhythms of grace. I won't lay anything heavy or ill-fitting on you. Keep company with me and you'll learn to live freely and lightly."

God created a rhythm of life – day and night, seasons, heartbeats – all moving to a set rhythm – and rest in Jesus is part of God's rhythm for our life.

Rest doesn't really get enough attention in our world. We seem to be talking about getting more done, achieving more and increasing productivity, but I think a pattern of resting is critical to fulfilling this need to get more done.

Time is one of the few things that everyone has the same amount of. It doesn't matter your age, race, background, country of birth – each week we all get 7 days and 24 hours in each day, to decide what we do with.

God showed us a pattern of using that time in the creation of the world. He worked for some time and then even made sure He made time for rest. The writer of the book of Hebrews put it this way, "There remains, then, a Sabbath-rest for the people of God; for anyone who enters God's rest also rests from their works, just as God did from His." (Heb. 4:9).

This word Sabbath means to rest from labour. When the Sabbath was adhered to in ancient times, the religious leaders added a lot of rules of what could and couldn't happen on a Sabbath, which Jesus regularly challenged. It was even a capital offense not to keep the Sabbath.

The first Christians kept the Sabbath, but originally on a Saturday. In AD 321 Constantine decreed that Sundays were an official public holiday and since then, Sunday has been the normal Christian day of rest and worship.

This Sabbath rest is thinking about how we order our time. The rest that we need for the sake of our health, our sanity, our spirituality, our relationships, and our community.

Sometimes you need to work hard at resting. Finding a time you can rest, and then guarding that time to make sure you get it. Make sure that in your rest you do things that are refreshing, for me that might be a game of golf or a surf.

Rest is a day when your work is done, even if it isn't. Rest is a time when you are fully available to yourself and those you love. Rest is a time when you produce nothing. Rest is a time when your only job is to enjoy.

Make sure that you enjoy other people in your rest – remember the most important things in life are not things, but people.

And finally, make sure that as Jesus has put in this command – we enjoy Him in our rest, He rested and created rest for us.

ACTION

What does rest look like in your weekly routine at the moment?
Do you need to make some changes to make rest a more regular pattern in your life?
How can you enjoy Jesus in your rest?

Thirty Two
Do not speak against the Holy Spirit

Key Reference: Matt. 12:31-33

Other References: Mark 3:29-33

NLT

"So I tell you, every sin and blasphemy can be forgiven - except blasphemy against the Holy Spirit, which will never be forgiven. Anyone who speaks against the Son of Man can be forgiven, but anyone who speaks against the Holy Spirit will never be forgiven, either in this world or in the world to come "A tree is identified by its fruit. If a tree is good, its fruit will be good. If a tree is bad, its fruit will be bad."

MSG

"There's nothing done or said that can't be forgiven. But if you deliberately persist in your slanders against God's Spirit, you are repudiating the very One who forgives. If you reject the Son of Man out of some misunderstanding, the Holy Spirit can forgive you, but when you reject the Holy Spirit, you're sawing off the branch on which you're sitting, severing by your own perversity all connection with the One who forgives. "If you grow a healthy tree, you'll pick healthy fruit. If you grow a diseased tree, you'll pick worm-eaten fruit.

The fruit tells you about the tree."

To get the full context of this command it's worth reading Mark 3 from verse 20. To give you a summary, Jesus is in a house and He and the disciples were inundated by a crowd and were not able to eat. Jesus' own family has started thinking He has gone mad and the religious authorities take the opportunity to suggest that what Jesus has been doing, is because He is filled with an evil spirit. Jesus starts to prove them wrong by an analogy of a civil war. Jesus makes it clear this is not a civil war, where Satan is fighting against himself – but a war that Jesus is entering, to take back humanity and to set people free.

It is within this context that Jesus gives the command about not speaking against the Holy Spirit and then likens the attitude towards the fruit of a tree. What the Pharisees did, that Jesus commanded against, was to label the work of the Holy Spirit as the work of the devil. It was a deliberate attitude of hostility against the power of God. The link to fruit helps us understand what Jesus was saying - the fruit in our lives reflects the attitudes in our heart. It's very similar to where Paul was talking about the fruits of the Spirit (Gal. 5:22-23). The fruit we bear in our lives is directly correlated to the seeds that we plant in our lives.

If we are planting seeds of faith and Kingdom living, this produces the fruits of the Spirit that Paul writes about: love, joy, peace, patience, kindness, goodness, faithfulness, gentleness and self-control. We can see from this command of Jesus, that the seeds being planted by the Pharisees, created an attitude so bad that they were trying to connect Jesus' work to that of Satan.

The fruit in your life can't be manufactured, it grows out of the unfolding journey of our lives. At a practical level, we can think about the seeds that we are planting and what kind of fruit it will produce. Consider what books you read, the movies you watch, the music you listen to and other things that you fill your mind with. What words do you use when you speak? How are you treating other people? What does your commitment to the things most important to you look like and what's the priority order of those things like your family, your church and your work? How do you start your day, as these are the first seeds you sow for the day?

When you catch behaviour in your life that you don't like, you can trace it back to seeds you're sowing, patterns that aren't in line with Kingdom living. You can't fake the fruit. It's not about striving, it's not about pretending, it's about living in and by the Spirit of God.

We don't have time to go through the full list, but there is a pattern to look at for each fruit. What is it, what is the opposite behaviour and what might it look like when we are trying to fake it? Let's consider love.

Love in this context is unconditional love. It's described as the love Jesus has for us, where He would lay down His life for ours. Think about it in the sense of serving someone, just because of their intrinsic value. The fake version of this is that we love someone because of what they might do for us or how their reciprocated love makes us feel about ourselves.

So this is a good chance to have a quick self-reflection. As my wife likes to say - the fruit of the Spirit is an outward reflection of an inward condition.

ACTION

Consider what seeds you are sowing in your life in the areas mentioned?
Are there seeds you are sowing, that are not in line with Kingdom living and bearing the wrong kind of fruit, that you need to consider changing?

Thirty Three
Do not speak careless words

Key Reference: Matt. 12:36-37

NLT

"And I tell you this, you must give an account on judgment day for every idle word you speak. The words you say will either acquit you or condemn you."

MSG

Let me tell you something: Every one of these careless words is going to come back to haunt you. There will be a time of Reckoning. Words are powerful; take them seriously. Words can be your salvation. Words can also be your damnation."

You might remember the small rhyme from when you were a child – "Sticks and stones may break my bones, but words will never hurt me." While the principle of not letting words impact us might be good, the reality is the words we use can be incredibly powerful for good and for bad and this rhyme is simply not true.

Here Jesus' command is to make sure we are accountable for the words that we use. It is estimated that the average human speaks around eleven million words in a year, so that's a lot of words to be accountable for!

James gave further warning on this, about the power of the tongue, which is worth reading, "For if we could control our tongues, we would be perfect and could also control ourselves in every other way. We can make a large horse go wherever we want by means of a small bit in its mouth. And a small rudder makes a huge ship turn wherever the pilot chooses to go, even though the winds are strong. In the same way, the tongue is a small thing that makes grand speeches. But a tiny spark can set a great forest on fire. And among all the parts of the body, the tongue is a flame of fire. It is a whole world of wickedness, corrupting your entire body. It can set your whole life on fire, for it is set on fire by hell itself." (James 3:2-6).

It can be said that we should think before we speak and a great acronym to help with that, as a filter before we speak, is "THINK".
T – Is it True?
H – Is it Helpful?
I – Is it Inspiring?
N – Is it Necessary?
K – Is it Kind?

We should use our words to encourage and uplift people. It is too easy to attack and hurt people with the things that we say, but we can use them to bless them, call out things that people are doing well or what we might see in their future. Our words can have a profoundly positive impact. Think about how you have felt when someone has given you a word of encouragement.

We should make sure our words are honest and truthful. Lying is something we can all do at times. It might seem like a white lie, or just bending the truth, a misleading hint or even silence, but it is all lying. I'm not sure why we do it but it seems we do. The cost of lying is that it often leads to more lying. It impacts our ability to distinguish between right and wrong in our own lives.

We should also refrain from using words that are about gossip. Gossip can be subtle, but it is very destructive in relationships. It's the "did you hear about..." conversation. Proverbs says: "A troublemaker plants seeds of strife; gossip separates the best of friends." (Prov. 16:28).

Let's be people of truth and encouragers, who avoid gossip and keep promises.

ACTION
Spend some time reflecting on the words you use?
Consider whether you need to repent from the wrong use of words through lies or gossip?
Where can you use your words today to encourage someone?

Thirty Four

Be on your guard against false teaching

Key Reference: Matt. 16:6-11

Other References: Mark 8:14-21

NLT

"Watch out!" Jesus warned them. "Beware of the yeast of the Pharisees and Sadducees." At this they began to argue with each other because they hadn't brought any bread. Jesus knew what they were saying, so He said, "You have so little faith! Why are you arguing with each other about having no bread? Don't you understand even yet? Don't you remember the 5,000 I fed with five loaves, and the baskets of leftovers you picked up? Or the 4,000 I fed with seven loaves, and the large baskets of leftovers you picked up? Why can't you understand that I'm not talking about bread? So again I say, 'Beware of the yeast of the Pharisees and Sadducees.' "

MSG

Jesus said to them, "Keep a sharp eye out for Pharisee Sadducee yeast." Thinking He was scolding them for forgetting bread, they discussed in whispers what to do. Jesus knew what they were doing and said, "Why all these worried whispers about forgetting the bread? Runt believers! Haven't you caught on yet? Don't you remember the five loaves of bread and the five thousand people, and how many baskets of fragments you picked up? Or the seven loaves that fed four thousand, and how many baskets of leftovers you collected? Haven't you realized yet that bread isn't the problem? The problem is yeast, Pharisee-Sadducee yeast." Then they got it: that He wasn't concerned about eating, but teaching - the Pharisee-Sadducee kind of teaching."

In this passage Jesus is talking directly about the false teaching at the time coming from the Pharisees and the Sadducees. Some of it originated based on who these people were in society and the way they pretended to be one thing, when in fact they were living for another.

To give some context, the Sadducees were aristocrats at the time, the wealthy high priests and chief priest. They held most of the seventy seats of the council called the Sanhedrin. They pretended to have a free search for their truth – but were aligned to Rome and were more interested in political alignment rather than religion.

The Pharisees were more like middle class businessmen. They had more contact with the common people. They had a minority of seats on the Sanhedrin but were more popular with support from the people. They were pretenders of devotion.

The analogy Jesus likens them to is yeast. Yeast is a type of fungus and if you add a little bit of it to bread it expands and keeps growing. He is saying their false teaching is like yeast. If it gets into something it gets to everything and expands.

The command is to be on guard against this kind of false teaching. We will hear false teaching, so we need to learn to discern which messages are false. The reality is that no one knows everything, so we all believe something now that is not true. Discovering truth is a lifetime endeavour but we need to avoid false teaching that has been dressed up as truth. This can happen when Scripture is misinterpreted and has an agenda behind it.

Let's look at how we can be on guard for this type of teaching. To know something is false you need to know the truth. Truth is found by knowing Jesus and by knowing His words. We need to be in regular relationship with Jesus – think about Him, seek Him, talk to Him and listen to Him. Jesus said "If you hold to my teaching, you are really my disciples. Then you will know the truth, and the truth will set you free." (John 8:31-32).

We need to learn to love reading the Bible. This is God's word and if you need to remember how we do this, go back to command 1 – Live on the Word of God. If you have concerns about some teaching you have heard, look at the fruit of the teacher's life over an extended period of time. Does it produce good fruit or is there a track record of ethical compromises.

Another way we guard against false teaching is through our faith in what Jesus has done in our lives before. These defining moments create the blocks in our faith foundation. They are when Jesus has revealed himself to us and enable us to remain steadfast in teaching that comes against that. Those faith blocks can be re-affirmed by thankfulness, so we need to make sure we spend time thanking Jesus for the things He has done in our past, knowing He is leading us into our future.

ACTION

Is there anything that you currently believe, that comes to mind, that you feel may have come from some false teaching?

Do you need to shift something in your day to give more time to Jesus and His word, so you are grounded in His truth?

What blocks have you built in your faith foundation from things Jesus has done in your past?

Thirty Five
Deny yourself

Key Reference: Mark 8:34-38

Other References: Matt. 16:24-28, Luke 9:23-27

NLT

Then, calling the crowd to join His disciples, He said, "If any of you wants to be my follower, you must turn from your selfish ways, take up your cross, and follow me. If you try to hang on to your life, you will lose it. But if you give up your life for my sake and for the sake of the Good News, you will save it. And what do you benefit if you gain the whole world but lose your own soul? Is anything worth more than your soul? If anyone is ashamed of me and my message in these adulterous and sinful days, the Son of Man will be ashamed of that person when He returns in the glory of His Father with the holy angels."

MSG

Calling the crowd to join His disciples, He said, "Anyone who intends to come with me has to let me lead. You're not in the driver's seat; I am. Don't run from suffering; embrace it. Follow me and I'll show you how. Self-help is no help at all. Self-sacrifice is the way, my way, to saving yourself, your true self. What good would it do to get everything you want and lose you, the real you? What could you ever trade your soul for? "If any of you are embarrassed over me and the way I'm leading you when you get around your fickle and unfocused friends, know that you'll be an even greater embarrassment to the Son of Man when He arrives in all the splendor of God, His Father, with an army of the holy angels."

We live in a world that is so much about self, we have literally created a new dialogue around the word selfie. This has come out of years of what I would call "isms" – consumerism, materialism, hedonism and individualism. The world around us wants instant gratification. If it feels good, then do it. We have the pursuit of pleasure and self-indulgence. We want to be who we want to be. We want what we want, when we want it. When we are so self-consumed, it makes it very difficult to follow the way of another King of our lives and it can make it hard to care for and minister to other people.

Our desires can be shaped by the world. If you listen closely to the advertising that is around you on the internet, the tv and the newspapers – it all speaks to your dissatisfaction. We are bombarded with phrases like you deserve this, or you need the bigger, faster, silkier, smoother, shinier version of this. It means we are never satisfied and when that reaches the most extreme point, it could be argued, that a lot of things wrong in the world come back to this – our wars, the environmental crisis, theft, adultery etc.

Paul wrote to Timothy about these last days and said "in the last days there will be very difficult times. For people will love only themselves and their money. They will be boastful and proud, scoffing at God, disobedient to their parents, and ungrateful. They will consider nothing sacred. They will be unloving and unforgiving; they will slander others and have no self-control. They will be cruel and hate what is good. They will betray their friends, be reckless, be puffed up with pride, and love pleasure rather than God. They will act religious, but they will reject the power that could make them godly. Stay away from people like that!" (2 Tim. 2:1-5).

Here Jesus is providing the counter-cultural command – to deny yourself. He phrases this around the concept of taking up your cross. We can often misunderstand this, thinking that we have a burden to carry – but a better meaning is to be willing to die to self, an absolute surrender. Here's some questions to help you consider that.

Are you willing to follow Jesus if it means:
- losing some of your closest friends?
- alienation from your family?
- the loss of your reputation?
- losing your job?
- losing your life?

So how do we deny ourselves and fight against the culture that is all about self? Awareness is a good start and thinking about how the desires of the world never deliver and only leave you wanting more.

We should try to find contentment in all circumstances. Live with an attitude of gratitude where we regularly practice thankfulness. Let God shape your desires. Be a generous giver and value relationships over things and tasks.

ACTION
Are there things that you are desiring that you know are not from God?
What do you think about the advertising that we are surrounded by?
How can you practically make changes in your life that show you are valuing God's desires over your own?

Thirty Six
Do not look down on little ones

Key Reference: Matt. 18:10

NLT

"Beware that you don't look down on any of these little ones. For I tell you that in heaven their angels are always in the presence of my heavenly Father."

MSG

"Watch that you don't treat a single one of these childlike believers arrogantly. You realize, don't you, that their personal angels are constantly in touch with my Father in heaven?"

The context of this command starts with Jesus' disciples asking Him who is the greatest in the Kingdom of heaven and He gave them an answer far different to what they were expecting. Jesus replied by saying that you need to humble yourself like a child to be great in the Kingdom of heaven. He then went on to caution us to not cause one of these little ones to sin.

In regards to little ones, there is dual meaning here for both children and also those who are young in the faith.

This command starts by telling us that the greatest is the humblest, the greatest is the lowest. Little children are the most vulnerable in our world, in the same way Christians early in their faith are the most vulnerable to not continuing in their journey.

When considering our own entry to heaven, this command is about humility. You don't come into the kingdom of heaven by your intellect. You don't come by your power and influence and you don't come by your birth or birth right. It is the humility and interest of a little child that is required for us to enter the kingdom of heaven. God chooses the humble and therefore we should not look down upon these people.

We can correlate this to Jesus' own life. When God came to earth, there are many forms His people were expecting at the time. He was the promised Messiah coming to save the Israelites, so the expectation was that He would have come like the priests or prophets or old, or maybe as a warrior ready to win the battle. But instead He came as a child. The most vulnerable and humble way He could have come.

Paul talks about this when he was writing to the Philippian church, "Don't be selfish; don't try to impress others. Be humble, thinking of others as better than yourselves. Don't look out only for your own interests, but take an interest in others, too. You must have the same attitude that Christ Jesus had. Though He was God, He did not think of equality with God, as something to cling to. Instead, He gave up His divine privileges, He took the humble position of a slave and was born as a human being. When He appeared in human form, He humbled himself in obedience to God and died a criminal's death on a cross. Therefore, God elevated him to the place of highest honour and gave him the name above all other names, that at the name of Jesus every knee should bow, in heaven and on earth and under the earth, and every tongue declare that Jesus Christ is Lord, to the glory of God the Father." (Phil. 2:3-11).

So, to not look down upon those that are the most vulnerable, as they are the greatest in heaven, is a discipleship moment to live with the humility of Christ. Our humility can be built by regularly thanking God for the goodness in our lives. To confess our sins regularly, realising the frailty of our humanity and that our salvation comes from Jesus. To learn from our mistakes. To listen to others. To always be a learner and ask questions. To always consider others before yourself.

ACTION

On reflection, are there people that you look down upon in any away that you need to repent of?

Are there patterns in your life that cause you to esteem yourself above others?

What changes do you need to make to live as humbly as a little child?

Thirty Seven

Go to other believers who sin against you

Key Reference: Matt. 18:15-17

NLT

"If another believer sins against you, go privately and point out the offense. If the other person listens and confesses it, you have won that person back. But if you are unsuccessful, take one or two others with you and go back again, so that everything you say may be confirmed by two or three witnesses. If the person still refuses to listen, take your case to the church. Then if He or she won't accept the church's decision, treat that person as a pagan or a corrupt tax collector."

MSG

"If a fellow believer hurts you, go and tell him - work it out between the two of you. If He listens, you've made a friend. If He won't listen, take one or two others along so that the presence of witnesses will keep things honest, and try again. If He still won't listen, tell the church. If He won't listen to the church, you'll have to start over from scratch, confront him with the need for repentance, and offer again God's forgiving love."

The intent in our Christian communities is to not sin against one another, but the reality of life and humanity is that we will. We come from different backgrounds, with different experiences and expectations, so as a community of believers trying to do life together there are going to be times when we have disagreements.

This means that conflict is inevitable, but it doesn't need to be a negative thing. It is often only through conflict that we have moments of growth in our own life. Unresolved conflict however can be very unhealthy and cause pain, offense and inappropriate behaviour in people for years to come.

This commandment echoes the earlier commandment 9 – to be reconciled.

The relational context between Christians is important. Not only are we living out Jesus' second greatest commandment – love your neighbour – but Jesus says that people will know we are His followers by our love for one another (John 13:35).

Our relationships should look different, but the problem is they often don't. A lot of the hurt in our lives comes from broken relationship. If we don't deal with it the right way, we can hold offense and unforgiveness. This impacts our behaviour which might mean we pull away from the church community, eventually leave church and it can extend to impacting our relationship with God. This is not the freedom that Christ died for and yet sadly, I have seen it happen so many times.

Jesus gives some very practical instructions here on how to deal with people who have sinned against you. In our church, when there have been these types of cases, we have followed these instructions literally and have seen some great restoration of relationship because of that. There are also some very practical thoughts on how to help deal with conflict that comes in relationships, that may help in these situations.

Make sure in any close relationship you have times of being thankful and appreciative of the other person. This builds a strong foundation to deal with conflict from.

Recognise the differences in other people. We are not all the same and that is a good thing. We all have our own personalities, quirks and styles and these are not points of conflict, just differences. In a thriving community, it can be these things that create a greater strength together than any individual alone.

When you find yourself in conflict, work for a resolution. That means there needs to be discussion and negotiation, not attack, surrendering or bargaining. If the conflict allows, try bringing God back into it by praying together. That can change a spiritual atmosphere where people are able to honour one another, forgive, act in humility and take the heat out of a situation that allows for resolution.

The final piece in conflict is forgiveness, but as this is the next command of Jesus we are looking at, we'll cover it then.

ACTION
As you search your heart, do you have unresolved conflict that you may need to try and resolve?
Is there a different way you can tackle that based on this command of Jesus?
How can you prepare yourself to better handle conflict in the future?

Thirty Eight
Forgive others

Key Reference: Luke 17:3

Other References: Matt. 18:21-35

NLT

"If another believer sins, rebuke that person; then if there is repentance, forgive. Even if that person wrongs you seven times a day and each time turns again and asks forgiveness, you must forgive."

MSG

"Be alert. If you see your friend going wrong, correct him. If He responds, forgive him. Even if it's personal against you and repeated seven times through the day, and seven times He says, 'I'm sorry, I won't do it again,' forgive him."

Forgiveness is the core message of the Bible.

It starts with the forgiveness that we have experienced in Jesus. We have all done things that separate us from God and will continue to into the future. Every thought, word and deed counts. Every time we do something that falls short of the perfection that God intended for us, we sin. The Good News of course is that Jesus died to save us from our sins. The blood that He shed is entirely about the issue of forgiveness and restoration.

As we repent of what we have done wrong, we are forgiven and restored to fulfil the purpose God has for us. Throughout your life, while you live in God's will, you will discover regular things that you need to change direction with, to repent from. That's part of what I love about journeying with God – there is always more. Repentance is a way of life, not a one-time event. If we truly repent, then we understand the weight of what we have been forgiven from. The result is a life that more and more reflects the character of Jesus as He forgives us, which then empowers us to fulfil this command and forgive others.

From the forgiveness we find in Jesus, we need to forgive others. In teaching us how to pray Jesus says, "Forgive us our sins, as we forgive those who have sinned against us." (Matt. 6:12).

Forgiveness is the release of resentment and anger towards someone who has harmed you, whether they deserve that or not. In doing so, it can help you move forward, rather than staying emotionally engaged in the injustice or trauma of the situation. It can shift feelings of anger and hurt into healing and peace.

We often find forgiveness hard because we feel like we are letting the offender off the hook. But if we truly understand forgiveness this doesn't have to be the case.

Forgiveness is not denying, approving or diminishing any sin caused against us, but it is leaving that for God to judge. That doesn't mean that we allow sin to occur over and over, and we should not keep ourselves open to ongoing sin against us, especially if that is any form of abuse. We can still hold people accountable for their actions.

Forgiveness doesn't mean you forget - forgive and forget is not a Scripture – but it does mean we choose to not let the sin influence how we interact with them. It means you want good for them. That you love them and even if it hurts emotionally, you still pursue good for them.

Forgiveness is not always the second part, you don't have to wait for someone to say they have wronged you, before you forgive them. Forgiveness is a choice.

Forgiveness is not a one-time activity, sometimes you have to forgive people over and over, which is what Jesus is referring to here – even seventy seven times. You might have forgiven, but if it bothers you again, you need to forgive again.

ACTION
Spend some time reflecting on the forgiveness that God has given you? Search your heart and see if there is any hurt or offense that you are holding onto, that you need to forgive someone from?

Thirty Nine
Use your money in a way that pleases God

Key Reference: Luke 18:18-25

Other References: Matt. 19:16-24, Mark 10:17-23

NLT

But to answer your question, you know the commandments: 'You must not commit adultery. You must not murder. You must not steal. You must not testify falsely. Honor your father and mother.'" The man replied, "I've obeyed all these commandments since I was young." When Jesus heard His answer, He said, "There is still one thing you haven't done. Sell all your possessions and give the money to the poor, and you will have treasure in heaven. Then come, follow me." But when the man heard this He became very sad, for He was very rich. When Jesus saw this, He said, "How hard it is for the rich to enter the Kingdom of God! In fact, it is easier for a camel to go through the eye of a needle than for a rich person to enter the Kingdom of God!"

MSG

You know the commandments, don't you? No illicit sex, no killing, no stealing, no lying, honour your father and mother." He said, "I've kept them all for as long as I can remember." When Jesus heard that, He said, "Then there's only one thing left to do: Sell everything you own and give it away to the poor. You will have riches in heaven. Then come, follow me." This was the last thing the official expected to hear. He was very rich and became terribly sad. He was holding on tight to a lot of things and not about to let them go. Seeing His reaction, Jesus said, "Do you have any idea how difficult it is for people who have it all to enter God's kingdom? I'd say it's easier to thread a camel through a needle's eye than get a rich person into God's kingdom."

God is not as concerned about your money as much as He is about you belonging to Him. You can't buy your way into heaven and you can't pay off your sin with money. Proverbs helps us understand this as it says, "The rich and the poor have this in common – the Lord made them both." (Prov. 22:2).

The rich young ruler seemed to have done everything he could to live a righteous life, but Jesus knew that in his heart of hearts, he had placed money and material wealth as a priority, to the point he was not prepared to give them up for the sake of following Jesus. We've already looked at the concept of mammon in command 17 – store up treasures in heaven – and this is an example of mammon at play.

Giving is one of the most tangible ways we worship God. Much of our life of worship – praying, reading the Bible, gathering with other Christians, doesn't come at a direct cost, in the same way giving money does. Really, we don't want to hold onto anything in this life more tightly than what Jesus wants and this is what He was challenging in the rich young ruler.

This starts with God's example that to care was to give. He gave His son Jesus to pay a price for us that means we can have eternal relationship with Him. So what does giving look like for us?

A starting point is to realise that everything belongs to God. Paul writes in Corinthians: "Now he who supplies seed to the sower and bread for food will also supply and increase your store of seed and will enlarge the harvest of your righteousness. You will be enriched in every way so that you can be generous on every occasion, and through us your generosity will result in thanksgiving to God." (2 Cor. 9:10-11).

If we think it is our money and things, then we also don't feel obligated to give it to anyone. If we realise that it is God's money and things – then our attitude shifts to think that I'm privileged and honoured that God would share with me, so that I can share some with others.

I love that this Scripture is about giving in a way that is thanking God. It is part of our worship. We don't give to get back from God, we give out of thanks and yet in doing so, God will continue to supply our seed, that we may continue to give – it's like a generosity circle.

Proverbs says, "Honour the Lord with your wealth and with the best part of everything you produce." (Prov. 3:9-10). Perhaps our challenge is not about how much we are giving away, but rather how much we are keeping for ourselves?

Don't wait until you have enough – but let's live with an attitude ready to give.

ACTION

How would you respond if God asked you to sell everything you had – honestly?

How do you feel about it being God who provides everything you have?

Is there anyone in need in your life right now that you need to be generous with?

Forty
Lead by being a servant

Key Reference: Matt. 20:26-28
Other References: Mark 10:41-45

NLT

But Jesus called them together and said, "You know that the rulers in this world lord it over their people, and officials flaunt their authority over those under them. But among you it will be different. Whoever wants to be a leader among you must be your servant, and whoever wants to be first among you must become your slave. For even the Son of Man came not to be served but to serve others and to give His life as a ransom for many."

MSG

He said, "You've observed how godless rulers throw their weight around, how quickly a little power goes to their heads. It's not going to be that way with you. Whoever wants to be great must become a servant. Whoever wants to be first among you must be your slave. That is what the Son of Man has done: He came to serve, not be served - and then to give away His life in exchange for the many who are held hostage."

Jesus never actually said to us that we need to serve. What He did, was say that we have been called to be served by Jesus.

He lived with the ultimate attitude of a servant heart and in that, set us an example of how we should live. As the King of creation, He could have come and said, "serve Me", but instead what He said to His disciples was "Follow Me". Do what I do.

We read many examples of His servant heart, such as washing His disciples' feet, caring for the poor, healing the sick and of course His greatest example, in giving His life as a ransom, a payment, to pay the price for our sin and death. Even in many non-religious leadership books, Jesus is set as the example of the servant leadership style. What other religious leaders have there been that have said "I will serve you"?

Many people who call themselves spiritual would claim that all the different religions are just different sides on the same mountain, climbing to find the same God. The problem with this, is that these other apparent Gods are all sitting at the top of the mountain waiting for us to find them, whereas our God is the only one that came down the mountain to meet us. God the Son, humbled himself as Jesus, to be with us on earth to serve us.

So our service then needs to be about following His example – serving God and serving others. It is our response to the freedom we have been given by Jesus serving us. When it comes to serving, we need to keep the attitude of a servant that just serves, even when no one is watching, and fight off the pride that says, "look at me as I'm serving other people."

Let's consider this as we get practical with what it looks like to follow Jesus' example of leading by being a servant, as well as the opposite spirit of "look at me".

Be willing to do any task. Real serving never distinguishes between the size of the tasks, in fact, even prefers the more menial tasks and is happy to go about it, even if there is no one else there.

A servant heart doesn't need feedback and is content if no one knows. The "look at me" version likes to be given the more important tasks and likes to do it in a public place where people can see. They require external feedback appreciating the effort they have put in.

Be willing to serve anyone. Jesus said in Mark 9:35 to be the servant of all. The "look at me" version likes to pick and choose who they serve and often because of what it may bring.

Be willing to serve all the time. A servant heart is a lifestyle, you are always ready to serve. The "look at me" version is temporary, often around a certain task and will pick and choose based on how you are feeling.

To follow Jesus' way is to excel in your serving and lead by being the best servant to God and others that you can be.

ACTION
What needs to change in your life to live with a servant heart all the time?
How do you feel Jesus has served you?
Who might you need to serve today?

Forty One
Seek humility

Key Reference: Luke 14:7-11

NLT

When Jesus noticed that all who had come to the dinner were trying to sit in the seats of honour near the head of the table, He gave them this advice: "When you are invited to a wedding feast, don't sit in the seat of honour. What if someone who is more distinguished than you has also been invited? The host will come and say, 'Give this person your seat.' Then you will be embarrassed, and you will have to take whatever seat is left at the foot of the table! Instead, take the lowest place at the foot of the table. Then when your host sees you, He will come and say, 'Friend, we have a better place for you!' Then you will be honoured in front of all the other guests. For those who exalt themselves will be humbled, and those who humble themselves will be exalted."

MSG

He went on to tell a story to the guests around the table. Noticing how each had tried to elbow into the place of honour, He said, "When someone invites you to dinner, don't take the place of honour. Somebody more important than you might have been invited by the host. Then he'll come and call out in front of everybody, 'You're in the wrong place. The place of honour belongs to this man.' Red-faced, you'll have to make your way to the very last table, the only place left. When you're invited to dinner, go and sit at the last place. Then when the host comes He may very well say, 'Friend, come up to the front.' That will give the dinner guests something to talk about! What I'm saying is, If you walk around with your nose in the air, you're going to end up flat on your face. But if you're content to be simply yourself, you will become more than yourself."

We live in a world where we are preoccupied with our image and our importance. The rise of social media has only added to this where we can regularly seek social approval for the successes we portray. Jesus speaks right to the heart of this in a very practical way. He demonstrates the quality of humility against the backdrop of pride, that has just surfaced at a dinner party over who would take which seat at the table.

Pride and humility are opposites and cannot co-exist. Pride is all about feeling more important than those around you. As C.S. Lewis says "As long as you are proud you cannot know God. A proud person is always looking down on things and people; and of course, as long as you are looking down, you cannot see something that is above you."

Humility is about being comfortable with who you are in the Lord and able to put others first. It's recognising that you can thank God for the gifts and talents He has given you, while still needing His help and knowing that you can't succeed in your own strength.

Humility is a character trait that we need to develop in our Christian journey. Referencing Proverbs, James writes: "God opposes the proud but shows favour to the humble." (James 4:6). Jesus himself said as part of the Beatitudes that God blesses those who are humble (Matt. 5:5).

Jesus is our perfect example of humility. His entire life represented humility and is expressed most when He as God, became man and died to pay the price that we were meant to pay.

This humility is best described by Paul in His letter to the Philippians: "Do nothing out of selfish ambition or vain conceit. Rather, in humility value others above yourselves, not looking to your own interests but each of you to the interests of the others. In your relationships with one another, have the same mindset as Christ Jesus: Who, being in very nature God, did not consider equality with God something to be used to his own advantage; rather, he made himself nothing by taking the very nature of a servant, being made in human likeness, and being found in appearance as a man, he humbled himself by becoming obedient to death— even death on a cross!" (Phil. 2:3-8).

To develop humility, we need to be comfortable with who we are in Christ. We need to be grateful for what we have. Be prepared to ask for help. Listen. Put others first.

A simple way to remember humility is with the acronym JOY:
Jesus first;
Others Second;
Yourself last.

ACTION

Are there any areas in your life that you have seen pride creep in?
What stands out to you about how Jesus lived with humility?
What changes can you put in your daily habits to develop humility?

Forty Two
Pay earthly taxes

Key Reference: Mark 12:14-17
Other References: Matt. 22:15-22, Luke 20:21-26

NLT

"Teacher," they said, "we know how honest you are. You are impartial and don't play favourites. You teach the way of God truthfully. Now tell us - is it right to pay taxes to Caesar or not? Should we pay them, or shouldn't we?" Jesus saw through their hypocrisy and said, "Why are you trying to trap me? Show me a Roman coin, and I'll tell you." When they handed it to him, He asked, "Whose picture and title are stamped on it?" "Caesar's," they replied. "Well, then," Jesus said, "give to Caesar what belongs to Caesar, and give to God what belongs to God." His reply completely amazed them.

MSG

They came up and said, "Teacher, we know you have integrity, that you are indifferent to public opinion, don't pander to your students, and teach the way of God accurately. Tell us: Is it lawful to pay taxes to Caesar or not?" He knew it was a trick question, and said, "Why are you playing these games with me? Bring me a coin and let me look at it." They handed him one. "This engraving—who does it look like? And whose name is on it?" "Caesar," they said. Jesus said, "Give Caesar what is his, and give God what is his." Their mouths hung open, speechless.

In day to day life there are all sorts of situations that we are faced with that require us to make small decisions. These quick decisions are often a representation of our values. Think of situations like whether you speed on the road, do you text while you are driving, do you pay bills on time or if you are short changed or under charged at the shop do you let them know?

Generally, God expects us to follow the law. Consider Paul's writing to the Romans, "Everyone must submit to governing authorities. For all authority comes from God, and those in positions of authority have been placed there by God. So anyone who rebels against authority is rebelling against what God has instituted, and they will be punished." (Rom. 13:1-2).

Now there are some occasions where breaking the law is ok, to be obeying God rather than the law. One instance could be when you are preserving someone's life, like the people who hid Jews in World War 2. Other instances might be where you are preaching the Gospel in a country that doesn't allow freedom of religion.

Here Jesus is giving us a command to obey the laws of the land. Caesar represents the government and that paying taxes to them is because they have some claims over us.

In our country I think sometimes we forget that the taxes go to great services that are about helping our community with things like education, health care, road maintenance and dealing with waste.

We need to remember that the government's claims over us are limited. Everything ultimately belongs to God and Jesus' command is helping us to understand that to give things to the government that belong to us, is an act of worship. Give to Caesar what is Caesars, but give to God what is Gods.

I think a lot of this relates to a general posture towards doing good. So much Scripture points to this: do not get weary of doing good, depart from evil and do good; let them see your good works and be rich in good works.

Perhaps a final way to understand this is based on what Peter says: "It is God's will that your honourable lives should silence those ignorant people who make foolish accusations against you." (1 Pet. 2:15). In other words, if we are leading someone to Jesus, the life they have watched us live doesn't detract from the message we are trying to bring.

ACTION
Are there any decisions you make that seem innocent but are actually breaking the law?
Are there any changes you need to make to ensure you are living an honourable life?

Forty Three
Love God with all your heart, soul, strength and mind

Key Reference: Mark 12:30

Other References: Matt. 22:37-38

NLT

Jesus replied, "The most important commandment is this: Listen, O Israel! The Lord our God is the one and only Lord. And you must love the Lord your God with all your heart, all your soul, all your mind, and all your strength."

MSG

Jesus said, "The first in importance is, Listen, Israel: The Lord your God is one; so love the Lord God with all your passion and prayer and intelligence and energy."

Right up front we need to recognise that Jesus says that this is His greatest commandment, so we need to make sure that we pay attention to this one and how we apply it to our lives.

If we translate the original words another definition could be – passion (kardia), prayer (psookhay), energy (ischus) and intelligence (dianoia).

Simply – love God with everything you have.

At a practical level let's start with the heart. The heart can often represent our passion and our emotions, to align our purpose with the kingdom of God (remind yourself of command 18 – Seek First the Kingdom Of God – for more on this).

Next we look at loving God with our strength. The Bible says that our body is the dwelling place of the Spirit of God. It's the physical casing God has given our spirit to do His work while we are here on earth – so we need to look after it. I'm not an expert on physical health, but I think we need to be a bit careful because the world gives us a lot of wrong information. We are presented with fads and quick fixes because ultimately food, diet and health is big business, so here's a couple of simple ideas.

Try to eat food as God intended it, like fresh fruit and vegetables, nuts, meat and avoid refined sugar, deep fried and processed food. Drink lots of water, every system in our body needs water, it flushes toxins out and carries nutrients to your cells. Exercise and stretch – many guidelines recommend thirty minutes, five times a week.

Next is love God with your mind. The Bible says that if anything is true, noble, right, pure, lovely, admirable, excellent and praise-worthy think about such things (Phil. 4:8).

Check what we are filling our minds with, the movies we watch, the books we read, the music we listen to.

We also need to give our mind time to rest. We live in a busy world so consider what your mind is doing when it is meant to be taking a break. God says for us to be still and know that He is God (Psalm 46:10). Try not to let your mind be ruled by guilt and condemnation, these things can bind you up. Jesus brings freedom and redemption which is the opposite to these things.

Finally, is to love God with your soul. Think about your inner self and your identity. The core part of us that defines our values, our decisions, our lifestyle and our behaviours. Consider how these line up with your faith context.

We've briefly touched on the aspects of loving God, but I'd encourage you to unpack each of these a lot more, to help your full being have daily habits that help you love God more.

ACTION

How can you make this commandment the one you orient your life around? What practical change can you make today to love God more with your heart, strength, mind or soul?

Forty Four

Love other people

Key Reference: Mark 12:31

Other References: Matt. 22:39

NLT

The second is equally important: 'Love your neighbour as yourself.'
No other commandment is greater than these."

MSG

And here is the second: 'Love others as well as you love yourself.'
There is no other commandment that ranks with these."

So here is Jesus' second greatest commandment. If we wanted to summarise all of His teachings it would be to love God and love other people. There is so much to say about this that I wrote a complete book on the topic called Love Love, that includes over 200 ways to practically love people.

The concept of loving people is such a Christian thing to say, so I like what Paul writes to the Roman church "Don't just pretend to love people... really love them." (Rom. 12:9).

The more that you learn to love God, the more you can't help but have a heart to love other people. The Bible says that God first loved us (1 John 4:7-12), so us loving other people is part of our response to God first loving us.

Our love for other people starts with loving other Christians. Jesus said, "Your love for one another will prove to the world that you are my disciples." (John 13:35). If we are unable to love other followers of Jesus, then it doesn't set a great example when we start reaching out to love other people. We are meant to look after other believers so that collectively our needs are being met, we are being cared for and supported on an emotional, physical and spiritual level. If a fellow believer is trying to reach out to love others, but is not in a healthy state themselves because of unmet personal needs, there is the possibility that in helping others they may negatively impact their own wellbeing.

There are so many other great Scriptures that talk about loving other people. Look at Isaiah 58, Romans 12 or 1 Corinthians 13 as a starting point. A lot talk about finding practical ways to love people.

By serving other people, by finding acts of love, we can practically demonstrate the love of God to them. It may get them to think about God in a different way, it could challenge their existing mind set, and in many cases, it may be the foundation of a relationship that begins and continues as we point people towards God.

The heart behind loving other people is a heart of generosity. It's about putting others before yourself, being prepared to use your own time and resources for the benefit of other people. Being generous with other people is one of the greatest examples we can give of demonstrating God's love to others.

If we really love people, then ultimately we want to see them in a relationship with Christ, knowing that at that point they will be able to live their life to the fullest, as their eternal future is secured.

ACTION

What simple but practical ideas do you have on how you can love other people?

Are there any fellow believers that you need to be caring for right now?

Who in your world could you practically love this week?

Forty Five

Be ready for Jesus to come again

Key Reference: Mark 13:32-37

Other References: Matt. 24:42-44, Luke 21:34-36

NLT

"However, no one knows the day or hour when these things will happen, not even the angels in heaven or the Son himself. Only the Father knows. And since you don't know when that time will come, be on guard! Stay alert! The coming of the Son of Man can be illustrated by the story of a man going on a long trip. When He left home, He gave each of His slaves instructions about the work they were to do, and He told the gatekeeper to watch for His return. You, too, must keep watch! For you don't know when the master of the household will return - in the evening, at midnight, before dawn, or at daybreak. Don't let him find you sleeping when He arrives without warning. I say to you what I say to everyone: Watch for him!"

MSG

But the exact day and hour? No one knows that, not even heaven's angels, not even the Son. Only the Father. So keep a sharp lookout, for you don't know the timetable. It's like a man who takes a trip, leaving home and putting His servants in charge, each assigned a task, and commanding the gatekeeper to stand watch. So, stay at your post, watching. You have no idea when the homeowner is returning, whether evening, midnight, cockcrow, or morning. You don't want him showing up unannounced, with you asleep on the job. I say it to you, and I'm saying it to all: Stay at your post. Keep watch."

End times is a topic that requires a lot of conversation. The Bible gives several indicators on what to expect and if you'd like to look at that more, check out Matthew 24 or the Books of Daniel and Revelation. With that said, my view is that we can get overly distracted by end times, where do we go, will our planet stay or go, what is the order of things, can we correlate current earthly events to biblical end time descriptions and more. The issue with this is that no one actually knows what will happen and our faith needs to remain consistent regardless of our end times theology. The reality is that Jesus is coming back at the exact time and way God wants it to happen.

This is where we need to understand the subtlety of Jesus' command here. He doesn't say to understand end times, He says to be ready for it. So what does it mean to be ready for Jesus to come again?

The command here is to be prepared. We need to be more excited about the prospect of Jesus coming again than we are of any earthly desire. You might have a great thing that is about to happen in your life in the next few months or years, but do you genuinely desire to see Jesus come back again before that thing happens? If not, maybe you've got too connected to something in this world.

Consider that if someone's eternal destiny is separation from God (what the Bible calls hell) then earth is the closest they will ever get to God, but if our eternal destiny is heaven, then earth is the furthest we will ever be from God. The first part of being ready is to make sure that we are holding things on earth loosely. The other aspect of being ready is about having an urgency for seeing others come to know Jesus. Think of the closest person you know right now who does not know Him. Think about your family, workplace, neighbours and community. If Jesus can come at any point, where are these people going? Once you know Him, while there is your own spiritual journey of maturity, there is one command that we know is true and that is to tell others about Him. You are obviously a smart person and have made an educated decision to follow Jesus (and I expect you wouldn't be this far through this book if you hadn't). So why not tell others about this way of life that you are following?

I think there is a counter argument to many of the reasons that people seem to want to wait to decide if they follow Jesus:
- maybe I'll do it later – but we know that relationships get better over time.
- maybe they have met other Christians and don't like what they see – but we are all broken people trying to journey in life and it is better together.
- maybe there are things in my past that I don't want to have to confront – but the core of Jesus message is about forgiveness.
- maybe it feels like there are so many rules to follow – but Jesus didn't come for rules, He came for freedom.

Maybe we even disqualify ourselves from telling others. Reasons like now's not the time, I'm too young, too old, I'm waiting until I finish my study, I'm waiting for the kids to grow up, I'm waiting until I get that promotion, and the list goes on. We have been given everything we need right now to tell others about Jesus. So if not you, then who? If not now, then when?

ACTION
Are there any things on earth that you feel you are holding on too tightly to?
Do you find you have developed your own excuses that are disqualifying you from telling others about Jesus?
Who in your world do you need to tell about Jesus this week?

Forty Six
Look after the least of these

Key Reference: Matt. 25:31-46

NLT

Then the King will turn to those on the left and say, 'Away with you, you cursed ones, into the eternal fire prepared for the devil and His demons. For I was hungry, and you didn't feed me. I was thirsty, and you didn't give me a drink. I was a stranger, and you didn't invite me into your home. I was naked, and you didn't give me clothing. I was sick and in prison, and you didn't visit me.' Then they will reply, 'Lord, when did we ever see you hungry or thirsty or a stranger or naked or sick or in prison, and not help you?' And He will answer, 'I tell you the truth, when you refused to help the least of these my brothers and sisters, you were refusing to help me.' And they will go away into eternal punishment, but the righteous will go into eternal life."

MSG

Then He will turn to the 'goats,' the ones on His left, and say, 'Get out, worthless goats! You're good for nothing but the fires of hell. And why? Because - I was hungry and you gave me no meal, I was thirsty and you gave me no drink, I was homeless and you gave me no bed, I was shivering and you gave me no clothes, Sick and in prison, and you never visited.' Then those 'goats' are going to say, 'Master, what are you talking about? When did we ever see you hungry or thirsty or homeless or shivering or sick or in prison and didn't help?' He will answer them, 'I'm telling the solemn truth: Whenever you failed to do one of these things to someone who was being overlooked or ignored, that was me—you failed to do it to me.' Then those 'goats' will be herded to their eternal doom, but the 'sheep' to their eternal reward."

I'd like you to think about the images of certain people groups that you might encounter. For each of these listed below – as you think about them try and catch the first thoughts that come to mind.

A homeless person, an elderly person, an indigenous person, someone who smokes, someone who is overweight, a Muslim person, someone who lives a homosexual lifestyle, a single person, a married couple, an immigrant, a refugee, a rich person or a poor person. The point here is that it is likely we have some prejudices that we live with, maybe conscious or sub-conscious.

In this command, Jesus is helping us understand that His Gospel message is for everyone and His heart is for those He describes as the least of these. He calls us to practically care for these people. This is a pattern right throughout Scripture with nearly four hundred passages that demonstrate God's concern for the orphans, the widows, the prisoners, the poor, the hungry, the sick and the disabled. At a very practical level we can ask ourselves these questions, that are just as relevant today as they were in Jesus' time on earth:

- when did you make a meal for someone that needed it?
- when did you open your home for someone that needed shelter?
- when did you supply clothes for someone that needed them?
- when did you last care for a sick person?
- when did you last visit someone in prison?

A nice summary of that is found in Micah where the context is God answering the question of how we show Him that we love Him. He says: "And what does the Lord require of you? To do justice, to love mercy and to walk humbly with your God." (Mic. 6:8).

To walk humbly is to know the heart of God, to be attentive to what He loves and desires and this command makes that clear in loving the least of these. We need to show people mercy, that is an attitude of unconditional grace and compassion. We need to show justice, that is to treat all people equally. In other words, we must do justice out of merciful love.

The Gospels that talk about Jesus' message very much focus on God's acceptance and forgiveness of sinners. The message is described as the Good News for the poor. We see story after story about those who have been marginalised by society. Stories like the tax collector, the crippled, the lame, the blind, the Samaritans and the women. It's a message that says salvation is the vertical positioning of the cross, covering every layer within our society. Today this extends to the refugee, the indigenous, the single parent, the fostered child and more. As the biblical narrative moves into Acts, we see the Gospel message moves from just Jerusalem to a geographical breadth into Judea, Samaria, to the Gentiles and to Rome. This breadth is the horizontal positioning of the cross.

This sets an example of how we should live – to take the Gospel that is vertically for everyone, to the horizontal breadth of all the earth, everywhere we go. Compelled by the surety of our salvation in Jesus, empowered by the Holy Spirit to respond with super-natural power to the will of the Father.

ACTION
Who represent the least of these in our society today?
Did you identify any prejudices you might have towards these people that you need help from God to overcome?
What practical way can you love "the least of these" this week?

Forty Seven

Celebrate communion (The Last Supper)

Key Reference: Matt. 26:26-29
Other References: Mark 14:22-26, Luke 22:14-23

NLT

As they were eating, Jesus took some bread and blessed it. Then He broke it in pieces and gave it to the disciples, saying, "Take this and eat it, for this is my body." And He took a cup of wine and gave thanks to God for it. He gave it to them and said, "Each of you drink from it, for this is my blood, which confirms the covenant between God and His people. It is poured out as a sacrifice to forgive the sins of many. Mark my words—I will not drink wine again until the day I drink it new with you in my Father's Kingdom."

MSG

During the meal, Jesus took and blessed the bread, broke it, and gave it to His disciples: Take, eat. This is my body. Taking the cup and thanking God, He gave it to them: Drink this, all of you. This is my blood, God's new covenant poured out for many people for the forgiveness of sins. "I'll not be drinking wine from this cup again until that new day when I'll drink with you in the kingdom of my Father."

What a profound moment, sharing the table with Jesus who sets in motion an event that has become a tradition, a reflection and a celebration for His followers throughout the generations.

The word communion means to share intimate thoughts and feelings at a mental and spiritual level, but to understand its full meaning requires a deeper exploration of the Passover meal that He was sharing with His disciples.

The Israelites, as God's chosen people, had been slaves in Egypt. God helped them escape by bringing ten plagues upon the Egyptians before Pharaoh eventually released them. The last of these was to kill the first born in each household. The Israelites were instructed to mark their homes with the blood of a lamb and then the Spirit of the Lord knew to Pass over these homes and not kill the first born. Passover became a Jewish festival that among other things, celebrated this moment that death passed over the Israelites, as God released them from slavery.

There is so much imagery in the festival regarding the readings that take place, the food that is eaten and more. We don't have time to cover it all here – but let's consider a few important things. In the original Passover God's people were saved by the blood of a lamb on their door. In this meal that Jesus is having with His disciples, they are celebrating Passover just before Jesus (who was also called the Lamb of God), was about to be crucified with His blood being shed to save all humanity.

The unleavened bread that Jesus breaks is to remember His body. The bread has no yeast which in parts of the Bible represents sin, so bread without yeast represents a holy God. The wine that Jesus drinks is part of four pouring's during the Passover meal. It is believed at the third pouring, known as the cup of redemption, where Jesus said this is my blood, confirms the covenant between God and His people. It is poured out as a sacrifice to forgive the sins of many.

Perhaps another way to look at this is His body, the Bread of life, signifies that Jesus is the one who provides all that we need. His blood represents the sacrifice that He made but also the New Covenant that we live under through Jesus' resurrection.

In the early church the celebration of communion took place in the homes of Christians. It was the opportunity to stop over a shared meal together and remember who Jesus was and what He has done, and that is something that we can still do today.

The Christian journey is meant to be done together. We learn from each other and we look after one another. We serve one another and we accept one another. We encourage one another and we spur each other on. So this command of Jesus, is a great opportunity to make sure that we are meeting together, sharing a meal and over that meal reminding each other that life is all about Jesus.

ACTION
What does the symbolism of communion mean to you?
What do you think of when you remember the body and the blood of Jesus?
Who can you have a meal with where you stop, have communion and remember Jesus together?

Forty Eight

Be Jesus' witnesses

Key Reference: Luke 24:45-48

Other References: Acts 1:8b

NLT

Then He opened their minds to understand the Scriptures. And He said, "Yes, it was written long ago that the Messiah would suffer and die and rise from the dead on the third day. It was also written that this message would be proclaimed in the authority of His name to all the nations, beginning in Jerusalem: 'There is forgiveness of sins for all who repent.' You are witnesses of all these things."

MSG

He went on to open their understanding of the Word of God, showing them how to read their Bibles this way. He said, "You can see now how it is written that the Messiah suffers, rises from the dead on the third day, and then a total life-change through the forgiveness of sins is proclaimed in His name to all nations - starting from here, from Jerusalem! You're the first to hear and see it. You're the witnesses."

As Jesus gets to the end of His time on earth, He starts reminding His disciples that they will be His witnesses. They need to remember all the things they have seen and heard and be ready to start telling others about it, to see His kingdom begin its advancement in the world.

We are also to continue to be Jesus' witnesses. We need to remember the things we have seen and the things that we have heard about Jesus. What are those moments in your life that Jesus has been so real for you? Those times that have created the strong foundations of your faith. These are the stories that we can testify to.

This command to be His witness is echoed after Jesus' resurrection in Acts where He says, "But you will receive power when the Holy Spirit comes on you; and you will be my witnesses in Jerusalem, and in all Judea and Samaria, and to the ends of the earth." (Acts 1:8).

It's in this Scripture that He gives us a strategy on how to be His witness. To start in Jerusalem, then to the neighbouring areas of Judea and Samaria and then to the ends of the earth.

Keep in mind that at this time, Jesus was talking to people who were Jewish, and Jerusalem was their hometown, and Judea and Samaria were neighbouring places. Each of these locations has a context of culture and geography.

Jerusalem was close geographically and they understood the culture well. This translates to our hometown, our friends, family and work colleagues. These are the people we have contact with in the course of everyday life, we speak their language and know their culture.

Judea was a place that had the Jewish custom but was not near Jerusalem – in other words they are people who share our culture and language – but are geographically more distant. They have the same socio-economic and ethnic background, but are not in our immediate network of relationships.

I live in Australia, so this could be people in other parts of Australia, or even countries that have similarities to us like England, New Zealand or Canada.

Samaria was a place that was very close, but the Samaritan people were culturally very different. For us this represents people who live in our society but might be from minority groups or have an indigenous heritage.

Finally, we get to the ends of the earth – people who are culturally and geographically distant from us.

So what does this mean for us? That the sharing of Jesus' message, to be His witness, is every Christian's mission across each of those cultural and geographical contexts.

Simply put – everyone, everywhere.

ACTION
What are the defining moments in your life with Jesus that you can testify to?
What does it look like for you to be Jesus' witness?
Who do you need to witness to and where do you need to do it?

Forty Nine
Receive God's power

Key Reference: Luke 24:49

Other References: Acts 1:8a

NLT

"And now I will send the Holy Spirit, just as my Father promised. But stay here in the city until the Holy Spirit comes and fills you with power from heaven."

MSG

What comes next is very important: I am sending what my Father promised to you, so stay here in the city until He arrives, until you're equipped with power from on high."

Throughout Scripture we see a pattern of what it was like when the Holy Spirit came and there was typically a context of fire and wind. You can read some of these examples in passages like God meeting Moses at Mt Sinai (Exod. 19:16-20) where God descended with fire. In the temple that Solomon completed when they carried the Ark of the Covenant into the Most Holy Place and fire came down from heaven (2 Chron. 7:1). When Elijah took on the prophets of Baal and the fire of God fell (1 Kings 18:36-39).

The Israelites were used to this imagery, but throughout Scripture until this point, the fire and wind of God encounters were about one person and for one point in time. What Jesus is referring to here is foreshadowing the Holy Spirit coming for all people, for all time.

In Acts 2 we read that this is the moment Jesus was referring to here, when the Holy Spirit came at Pentecost and did so in what is described as tongues of fire and the sound of a blowing wind – the same imagery we have seen throughout the Bible to this point.

When John was writing to some of the early churches, he said that if we want to be a follower of Jesus, we need to live like Jesus lived (1 John 2:6).
Jesus also said that if we follow His life, we will be able to do even greater things than He has done (John 14:12). When you stop and think about that, it's almost impossible to comprehend. Jesus raised people from the dead, healed thousands of people, cast out demons, walked on water, fed thousands of people from a few loaves of bread and some fish, turned water into wine, loved people who were outcasts of society and so much more.

But it's because of the Holy Spirit that we can do all the things that Jesus did and more. Jesus said that we will receive power when the Holy Spirit comes upon us (Acts 1:8). That's the same power that Jesus had, a supernatural power that allows us to live like Jesus in this world. Paul writes "for the kingdom of God is not a matter of talk but of power." (1 Cor. 4:20).

This command is to receive the Holy Spirit. A supernatural power is part of this but the Bible also says that the Holy Spirit guides us into truth (John 16:13), He is our counsellor and teacher (John 14:26), He leads us (Rom. 8:14) and is there for us in times of weakness and prayer (Rom. 8:26).

Part of our relationship with God is learning to hear and respond to the Holy Spirit. My experience is that He communicates with the senses He created us with, hearing, seeing and feeling. I have heard from God through creation, from other people, in my prayer times with him, through Scripture and through dreams. I want to encourage you to have a belief that God will speak to you and that He will demonstrate His power through you.

ACTION

What do you think it means to be filled with the power of the Holy Spirit?
What experiences have you had where you have seen the tangible presence of God?
Knowing that God the Spirit lives within you, how might you live differently today?

Fifty

Make and baptise disciples

Key Reference: Matt. 28:19-20

Other References: Mark 16:16, John 17:20-23

NLT

Therefore, go and make disciples of all the nations, baptizing them in the name of the Father and the Son and the Holy Spirit. Teach these new disciples to obey all the commands I have given you. And be sure of this: I am with you always, even to the end of the age."

MSG

God authorized and commanded me to commission you: Go out and train everyone you meet, far and near, in this way of life, marking them by baptism in the threefold name: Father, Son, and Holy Spirit. Then instruct them in the practice of all I have commanded you. I'll be with you as you do this, day after day after day, right up to the end of the age."

Jesus' final command to us was to go and make disciples. In reaching our last command we've completed a full circle because it is here that Jesus says to make disciples we must teach them all the commands He has given, which is what we have done over these last fifty devotions.

The word disciple means to learn or to be a follower of a teacher. As a Christian, this is a call on everyone, to make and baptise disciples. It's not the job of the professional minister or pastor, it's the role of every Christian. Jesus has made you compatible with the way He has called you to live, so while there are things you can learn, if you are already a follower of Jesus you are also equipped to do this.

Paul puts it this way as He says, "Follow me as I follow Christ" (1 Cor. 11:1). It's a relational context that says I'm following Jesus, so just imitate me and I'll help you do the same thing. Of course, this does require us to look at our own life to reflect on how we are following Jesus. If we can recognise and accept who Jesus is then we make disciples by positioning ourselves behind Jesus and allowing others to follow the patterns of our lives.

Jesus was the best disciple maker because He taught His disciples to reproduce the discipleship process in others. We see this with the early advancement of the church to thousands of people, six million people by the end of the second century and now at an estimated one third of the world's population. This didn't happen because of modern media techniques, it was about Christians sharing their message with their most immediate network of friends and family and fulfilling this command of making disciples.

Jesus' discipleship was a process that can be learned and repeated. First of all, it was relational. Most of the lessons He taught were done in the context of His disciples doing life together. In a healthy relationship communication is easy, spending time together is easy, sharing problems is easy, trust is easy, serving is easy – all of which to say, following is easy, but it must come out of relationship.

Jesus' discipleship pattern was intentional. If you think about it they were together a lot. They went to parties together, shared meals together, travelled together, fished together, prayed together and the list goes on. In so many of these situations Jesus would teach out of everyday life as if class was always on.

His discipleship was incremental. Each lesson seemed to build on the last and He would often get them into growth situations (see Luke 9:1-6). We see this where in one place in the Gospels they are unable to cast out a demon (Matt. 17:19) and yet later in Acts we seem them having learned that lesson and being able to do it (Acts 16:16-18).

Remember that discipleship is about the individual. Jesus himself was only able to focus on twelve people at the level of relationship that was required. While there is a model to follow in Jesus' discipleship, let's make sure we don't lose sight of the importance of the one to one relationship, and that each person we disciple is a unique individual.

ACTION

Is there someone in your life that has discipled you?

What are some of the lessons we can learn from the way Jesus discipled?

Who do you think you can now disciple and teach the commands of Jesus to?

Conclusion
Jesus said it

So, as we conclude our devotional series together you've made it through a study that has allowed you to reflect on the things that Jesus has commanded.

When Jesus gave His Two Greatest commandments, they make so much more sense now. To love God with everything you have and show that love to everyone else, everywhere you go almost encapsulates the fifty commands we have just studied.

His final command is the final challenge of this book. We are to be disciples who make disciples, teaching them to obey the commands that Jesus taught.

Who is it that you are discipling, that you can teach these commands to?

Don't now just put this book on your shelf. Why not give it to someone that you are discipling, so they can have the opportunity to go and study Jesus' commands too.

Thanks for reading.

About the author

Derek has spent 20 years living at the intersection of work and faith.

He has a Bachelor of Business and a Master of Arts in Christian Studies.

Derek is the Senior Minister at the church he and his wife Kylie planted - Local Community Church in Western Australia (www.localcommunity.church).

On a business front, Derek has built and sold a number of businesses, facilitated over $50m of venture funding, and advised 100's of companies in his roles as an Entrepreneur-In-Residence, Investor, Board Member and Advisor.

You can find out more or contact Derek at: www.derekgerrard.com

Derek is also the author of the following books available on his website:
- Love Love (Don't just pretend to love people... really love them)
- Christian Stuff
- The Church Startup
- Maximus the dog and his ~~tails~~ tales that teach us about God (an illustrated Children's book)

Notes

Notes